The Four Commands of Christ

James E. Ford

Publishing Services provided by Paper Raven Books LLC

Printed in the United States of America

First Printing, 2022

Hardback ISBN: 979-8-9857687-1-8
Paperback ISBN: 979-8-9857687-2-5
Ebook ISBN: 979-8-9857687-01

This book is dedicated to my family, who gave me insight, moral support, and sometimes exciting conversations, and to Steve and Leslie Rice, friends who supported me when I was floundering.

Table of Contents

Definitions v

Introduction ix

History of the Commandments xiii

The Four Commandments of Christ™ xxiii

──────── *Part One* ────────
The Four Commands of Christ

Chapter One
First Command: Humble Yourself and Submit 1

Chapter Two
Second Command: Give Grace and Mercy 17

Chapter Three
Third Command: Practice Forgiveness
within Your Church 23

Chapter Four
Fourth Command: Live Your Mission 31

──────── *Part Two* ────────
Spiritual Disciplines

Chapter 5
Know You Are Eternal 47

Chapter 6
Commit to Jesus 53

Chapter 7
Get on Your Knees and Pray 61

Chapter 8
Read Your Bible 69

Chapter 9
Memorize Scripture   73

Chapter 10
Tithe Your Money   79

Chapter 11
Tithe Your Time   85

Chapter 12
Thank God Always   89

Chapter 13
Fasting   95

Chapter 14
Be Disciplined   99

Chapter 15
Find Strength in Your Weakness   105

Chapter 16
Examine Yourself   109

Conclusion   117

Definitions

Being in the Zone When you are living a holy life.

Born Again To believe that Jesus is the Son of God and accept Jesus into your heart.

CHRINO Christian In Name Only; No substance to your faith or walk. Formalism.

Christian Perfection Striving to be like Jesus. Christian perfection is to have the attitude of Christ in faith, love, and circumcision of the heart. Humbling yourself and submitting to God is the beginning of the road to Christian perfection and continual improvement. It is not our works that pleases God but our heart attitude that pleases Him as we do His commands.

Corporate Prayer When two or more are gathered from the body of Christ and pray together.

Disciple A follower or student of a teacher, leader, or philosopher. A follower of Jesus Christ who does His will.

Discipleship   Equipping Christians so they can successfully live according to Christ's teachings, training them to duplicate His teachings.

End Times   A point and time in history as described in Revelations, Daniel, and Matthew in what will happen here on Earth just before Jesus comes for His people, which is coined the rapture.

Fuego   *Fuego* is Spanish for fire and in my terms means the following:
—A fire that burns inside you when you are filled with the Holy Spirit
—A fire, from the Holy Spirit, that fills and drives you to Holiness
—An all-consuming fire

Governing Value   Anything that you put your money, time, energy, and effort into.

Intercessory Prayer   When a Christian prays on behalf of another person to God.

Praising Prayer   Lifting up Christ to His rightful inheritance. Glorifying Christ and God.

Sanctification   To be set apart for God's design and purpose.
The act of making or declaring something holy.
The work of God which transforms believers into the likeness of Christ.
The action or process of being freed or purified from sin.

Sin   Any willful disobedient act that separates you from your relationship with God.

**Thankful
Prayer**

Thanking God for any and all reasons all the time.

The Elect

Anyone who has accepted Jesus Christ as his/her Savior and King and then lives according to His Scriptures.

The Lost

Anyone who has not been born again.

Introduction

As I sit here trying to figure out how to start a book that God has put the content of in my heart, I wonder who am I to even write a book. I am not a scholar, nor am I a pastor or a missionary. I am a carpenter (seriously), trying to relay what Christ wants everyone to know about His Kingdom. I may not know the first thing about writing a book, but I am confident of what Jesus has asked me to share with you.

Some of what I am going to say may seem harsh and biased. All I can say is that I hope you read it to the end before evaluating the points I am making here. After reading the book, all you have to do is make one decision about which road you choose to take: the wide road or the straight and narrow road. I pray that each one of you decides to take the narrow road, the road that leads to life. You may find yourself thinking, "I have tried and tried, only to find short-term success before I fall again." You may feel tired and want to be left alone. Those of us who empathize with this feeling can find help in this book. We have all been there at one point and time in our life. I have probably been at this point hundreds of times in my life. I was so tired of failure that I cried out to God for a way to win this struggle for my soul. The Apostle Paul also describes this situation I was going through in Romans 7:16-24.

One afternoon, God shared with me His answer to the question I had asked Him. He showed me simple instructions for those who will listen. The Four Commands of Christ changed my life. They told me how to live, how to behave, and how to worship. All the commands are love and teach us how to practice His love. His message carries the keys to life. He asked me to share His will for us in times such as these. How do you refuse such a request from God? I know who called me and what He wants me to share because He put it in my heart, mind, and soul. I know His voice and His calling. I have heard it said, "If not me, then who?"[1] Jesus said to me, "Who will go forth and tell My people that they need to turn from their misguided ways and return to Me?" He also informed me that I am called to do this in Ezekiel 3:17: *"Son of man, I have made thee a watchman unto the house of Israel: therefore, hear the word at my mouth, and give them warning from me."* This book is about waking up all the people of the world who will heed the warning of the coming difficulties when we lose our freedom to worship Jesus openly and freely. As Christians, or people who may be sitting on the fence, we need to focus on what is important to Christ to make sure we are ready for the end times. Something we should ask ourselves is who is God talking to when He said,

> *"Not everyone that saith unto me, Lord, Lord, shall enter into the kingdom of heaven; but he that doeth the will of my Father which is in heaven. Many will say to me in that day, Lord, Lord, have we not prophesied in thy name? and in thy name have cast out devils? and in thy name done many wonderful works? And then will I profess unto them, I never knew you: depart from me, ye that work iniquity."* (Matthew 7:21-23 KJV)

What causes sincere believers to fall away from God? Could it be that they don't spend enough time in the spiritual disciplines and fall prey to sin nature elevated by Satan's lies? When we pray and our prayers are not answered on our timetable, do we become discouraged and find a solution on our own? Satan seems to be able to frame our issues so they become complicated, and when you come to your wit's end, you cave. You cave because you do not understand God's ways,

---

1 Hillel

and you have not maintained that personal relationship with Christ. So, you go the way of the crowd. A single, small sin—or a white lie as we sometimes look at it—causes us to be separated from the Holy Spirit.

Could it be these issues come along because we are not spending enough time with God and obeying His commands? Do we see the Glory of God working in our lives or in other Christians' lives? We hear of Christian singers and personalities falling away from the faith all the time. Why? Maybe they are not living the faith consistently, or there is too much temptation in front of them, so they sin. They allow too many sinful ideas, thoughts, actions, and speech into their lives.

There are too many distractions available to us now. It is so easy to get sidetracked with technology and spend an unhealthy amount of time with our devices instead of with Christ. If we would put aside our toys and give God that time, what would our relationship with Him look like? So many people, including people of faith, are so busy with life that they don't have time for Christ. People go to church and participate in church activities, but some still go home empty inside. They follow the rules, and maybe they are even strict in following rules, yet they are all still lacking.

When we see churches failing and growing cold, why is this happening? Could it be a lack of a firm foundation and discipleship programs that deepen relationships with Christ? We teach about sin, but are we teaching how to overcome sin? Are we teaching how to live holy lives and be successful Christians?

It is more than simply knowing Christ. It is about loving Christ, serving Christ, surrendering to Christ, and maintaining that relationship with Him. Tithing your time is how I describe this. Jesus said we should love the Lord God with all of our heart, mind, soul, and strength. The topics in this book will give you the tools you need to have that personal relationship with Jesus so you can experience Peace. *Shalom Adonai.*

The Four Commands of Christ will give you the *fuego*—the spiritual fire—to spread the Good News of Christ. If we continue in this practice, we can then increase the number of people in the faith and quickly at that. Think about it: If all of us would work at spreading the Good News instead of leaving it to the church staff or missionaries, what would our town or city look like in two years? Many Christians believe this is meant for the church to undertake and not the individual. I am telling you it is all of our jobs to spread the Good News of Christ.

The Four Commands of Christ is about applying these holy principles to your life. There are only four, and they are not difficult to understand. They are simple and to the point. In Exodus 18:20, Jethro tells Moses, *"Teach them His decrees and instructions and show them the way they are to live and how they are to behave."* In this book, I hope you see what I see in the Four Commands of Christ. They come directly from Jesus to you and me. During one of the many long conversations my son Brent and I have had, he came up with a brilliant quote. He said, *"Knowledge alone is not power; knowledge applied is power. If you want power in your relationship with Jesus, then you need to apply the knowledge you are learning."* This book has two goals: to help those struggling move toward a solid relationship with Christ and to help the nonbeliever find Christ and have purpose, love, and joy. My vision is for everyone to learn how to be a successful Christian. If everyone would adopt and practice The Four Commands of Christ worldwide within all denominations, what a difference this would make. I want everyone to join me at the banquet dinner in heaven. In Matthew 22:30 Jesus says, *"At the resurrection people will neither marry nor be given in marriage; they will be like the angels in heaven."* We will all be like angels, and we will not belong to any denomination. We will all be God's children.

There will be no denominations in heaven. Let's all adopt the Four Commands of Christ and change the world for Christ!

Fuego

History of the Commandments

In order to understand the Four Commands of Christ, we must start at the beginning. In providing my version of the history of the Ten Commandments, please know that I am not trying to portray myself as a historian or a Biblical scholar, as I am far from being either. Forgive me for any points that will be missed and know that some of my writing is inspired by God, and other aspects of my writing are based on my experience and knowledge. I am sure of this: I am moved by the Spirit, and I need to write to fulfill the calling that Christ gave me.

God gave Moses the Ten Commandments to rule and govern over the new nation of Israel. They were held captive in Egypt for 430 years by the time Moses led them out. It is a great story of how Abraham, Isaac, Jacob, and then Joseph and the Hebrew people came into existence. (You can read it in Genesis.) Jacob and his children migrated to Egypt because of a famine in the land of Canaan. They were saved from this famine because of a dastardly deed committed by all of Joseph's brothers, except one, when Joseph was young. Joseph's brothers sold him into slavery after Judah talked them into it. The other brothers were intent on killing him. The person who bought Joseph resold him to Potiphar in Egypt. Joseph was found to be a very capable and handsome young man, so Potiphar put Joseph in charge of all that he owned except his wife. Now, Potiphar's wife was putting the moves on Joseph, but he always refused. One day, she caught him off guard and grabbed him; he escaped by slipping out of his overcoat. Potiphar's wife falsely accused Joseph of assault, so Potiphar had him jailed.

In jail, Joseph had become known by his fellow inmates as a dream interpreter. Two of Joseph's inmates had dreams and were perplexed because no one could interpret them. Joseph asked, "Don't interpretation of dreams come from God?" So, he interpreted the baker's dream and said that he would lose his life within three days. After three days, both the baker and cupbearer were called before Pharaoh, and the baker was killed and the cupbearer restored. Sometime later, Pharoah had a dream, and the cupbearer remembered Joseph and his unique abilities. Joseph was called before Pharaoh to interpret the dream. Through God's help, Joseph interpreted Pharaoh's dream and became prominent in Egypt. Joseph ruled Egypt, with only Pharaoh holding a higher station of prominence and power.

In interpretating Pharaoh's dream, Joseph knew that there would be seven years of plenty and seven years of famine. Joseph stored up grain seven years, and when the famine hit, the only way to acquire food was through Egypt.[2] After some jostling by Joseph against his brothers, he finally asked his family to come to Egypt and settle in the land of Goshen during those famine years. This is how Israel (Jacob and his family) came to Egypt. Why they decided to stay there and not go back home to the land of Canaan is a mystery. Maybe, like Abraham's father, they liked the land that they had settled into and the favors they received at that time. They forgot their calling.[3]

Sidebar here: Have you felt like you have lost your passion for Christ? Lost your first love?[4] Why do we enjoy a season of sin and disdain a day with Jesus? We seem to enjoy this season of sin and feel comfortable in it; then, one day, it sneaks up on us and enslaves us.[5] We should learn from Israel's mistakes and make sure we keep our eye on the goal—heaven—by glorifying God.

Now back to the story. We need to remember that Israel was in Egypt for 430 years and not living where God had intended them to live after the promise God had given Abraham, Isaac, and Jacob. I should preface

2 Genesis 41:39-49
3 Genesis 11:31
4 Revelations 2:4
5 James 1:13-15

that the people living in the Promised Land at this time had not yet reached their full involvement in sin yet. It took the occupants of the Promised Land 430 years to reach a point where God had had enough. After some time living in Goshen, they fell into slavery at the hands of one of Egypt's Pharaohs (possibly Thutmose I), who did not recognize Joseph's part in the history of saving Egypt from famine. Exactly when that happened is a matter of conjecture.

After a great deal of time in slavery, Moses was born. It was a terrible time to be born a Hebrew. The current Pharaoh had sent out an order to kill all newborn males born of Hebrew women with the aim of reducing the Hebrew population, whose numbers were quickly overwhelming the Egyptians. Moses's mother, however, refused to turn him over to be killed by the Egyptians and instead made a basket of reeds and sent him down the Nile River. That journey on the Nile in a reed raft left Moses's fate in God's hands.

Moses was the son of Hebrew slaves and was saved from death by Pharaoh's daughter, whose handmaiden found him stuck in the reeds by their bathing spot. The Egyptian princess brought him out of the Nile and adopted Moses as her own son. Moses grew up knowing he was a Hebrew but also an Egyptian royal prince. The adopted son of Pharaoh's daughter grew up in a position of power, education, and prominence; Moses became one of the princes of Egypt. However, he would eventually trade in his royalty for who he really was: a Hebrew, an Israelite.

After watching an Egyptian guard mistreating one of his fellow Hebrews, Moses sought out that guard and killed him. He was later found out by Pharaoh and ran away from Egypt to evade death. Moses eventually settled in Midian and married a Midianite Priest's daughter. Moses's father-in-law, Jethro, was a Midian priest before the Lord. Moses decided to stay in that land. As a shepherd for his father-in-law, he tended flocks of sheep. Then, one day, God called to him from a burning bush on Mt. Sinai. Somehow, the bush was not consumed by the fire, which captured his attention. He drew closer to the bush. God called to him again. He said, *"Moses, remove your sandals for this is holy ground."* God told Moses that he wanted him to go back to Egypt and free His people. Moses was reluctant, just like all of us are when God sends us on a mission. Moses made all kinds of excuses but finally went with his brother, Aaron, to free God's people, his fellow Hebrews, the Israelites.

When Moses arrived in Goshen, an area of Egypt where they settled when Joseph ruled Egypt, he told the prominent men of Israel what God had told him to tell Pharaoh. The leaders of Israel were reluctant to agree. He had to convince the leaders that God had sent him to free them from bondage and take them to the Promised Land. After Moses showed them the miracles God used to prove He had called Moses, they agreed. The message God gave Moses to tell Pharaoh was, *"Free my people so we may worship our God."* Moses knew full well that this would fulfill the promise God had made to Abraham. So began his ministry.

When Moses finally approached Pharaoh, he said, *"Let my people go, so that they may hold a festival to me in the wilderness"* (Exodus 5:1). Pharaoh refused and made their life even harsher. Moses approached Pharaoh nine times. Each time Pharaoh refused to release the Hebrews, God would send a plague. After the ninth time, one last terrible plague came, bringing the death of the firstborn son of every family living in Egypt unless the blood of a lamb was present over the front of the entry doorpost. Moses had all the Hebrews put blood over their doorposts so the death angel would not visit their firstborn sons, as God had told him to do. This last plague against Pharaoh and the people of Egypt came to be known as the Pesach, a major annual Hebrew celebration called the Passover. Celebrating this every year is one of the requirements God gave Moses to have the Nation of Israel to follow.

> *"This is how you are to eat it: with your cloak tucked into your belt, your sandals on your feet and your staff in your hand. Eat it in haste; it is the Lord's Passover. On that same night I will pass through Egypt and strike down every first-born of both people and animals, and I will bring judgment on all the gods of Egypt. I am the Lord. The blood will be a sign for you on the houses where you are, and when I see the blood, I will pass over you. No destructive plague will touch you when I strike Egypt." (Exodus 12:11-13)*

Pharaoh finally let the Hebrews go. Soon after, though, he changed his mind and went after them with his army. This proved to be a disastrous mistake as Pharaoh and his army were swallowed up by the Red Sea. Egypt's written records do not say how this Pharaoh was killed, nor do they speak of the Hebrews being freed. Israel was finally free to worship God. We have come to know this story and all of the great miracles that God performed on behalf of the Hebrews in their Scripture called the Torah.

On the way to the Promised Land, God had the Hebrews camp at Mt. Sinai. It was here that God told Moses to come up to the mountain and write down His instructions for Israel. It was the same mountain where God had sent him to free Israel. God Himself wrote the Ten Commandments on the two stone tablets carved out by Moses. The first four commandments relate to our personal and corporate relationships to God (man to God). The other six commandments are about our relationships to each other (man to man). These are sets of laws and decrees that God instructed Israel, and by extension us, to live by. Israel is the first and only nation to carry God's written laws. Without that journey, as told by Moses, of what God did for Israel, we would not have the Old Testament or God's laws as written in what is called the Pentateuch (the first five books of the Bible, which are part of the Torah). The two stones with the Ten Commandments were eventually stored in the Ark of the Covenant, along with the manna from heaven and Aaron's budded staff.

God appointed Israel as a priestly nation, setting the example for all of us for how to live and how to behave.[6] Israel was also the nation through which Jesus, the Messiah, came so all of us could be saved. As Paul tells it, the Hebrews were first, and we gentiles are grafted into that religion through Christ. The Hebrew ruling party rejected their Messiah and crucified Him on the cross, and so we gentiles were grafted into God's grace by accepting Christ into our hearts. This is how our Judeo-Christian basis of laws and morality came about. The United States was founded on such rules, laws, and moral ethics.

---

6 Exodus 19:6

Here are the Ten Commandments using the King James Version, with its eloquent style that reads larger than life.

The First Four Commandments (Exodus 20:2-11):

"I am the Lord thy god, who brought thee out of the land of Egypt, out of the house of bondage.

Thou shalt have no other gods before me.

Thou shalt not make unto thee any graven image, or any likeness of anything that is in heaven above, or that is in the earth beneath, or that is in the water under the earth. *Thou shalt not bow down thyself to them, nor serve them: for I the Lord thy God am a jealous God, visiting the iniquity of the fathers upon the children unto the third and fourth generation of them that hate me, and shewing mercy unto thousands of them that love me and keep my commandments.*

Thou shalt not take the name of the Lord thy God in vain; *for the Lord will not hold him guiltless that taketh his name in vain.*

Remember the Sabbath day, to keep it holy. *Six days shalt thou labor and do all thy work: but the seventh day is the Sabbath of the Lord thy God: in it thou shalt not do any work, thou, nor thy son, nor thy daughter, thy manservant, nor the maidservant, nor thy cattle, nor thy stranger that is within thy gates. For in six days the Lord made heaven and earth, the sea, and all that in them is, and rested the seventh day, wherefore, the Lord blessed the Sabbath day, and hallowed it."*

The Next Six Commandments (Exodus 20:12-17):

"Honor thy Father and thy Mother: that thy days will be long upon the land which the Lord thy God giveth thee.

Thou shalt not kill.

Thou shalt not commit adultery.

Thou shalt not steal.

Thou shalt not bear false witness against thy neighbor.

Thou shalt not covet thy neighbor's house, thou shalt not covet thy neighbor's wife, nor his manservant, nor his ox, nor his ass, nor anything that is thy neighbor's."

These commandments have been Jewish written law in the Torah for over 3,500 years. God has always instructed His people in His ways if they would only listen. Yet people living both in modern and ancient times only listen to what they want to (hence, the reason for the flood). Christians water down God's written word or remove it completely from our lives when we don't have a relationship with Christ. When people do not know God's laws or His word and only know a part of His laws, our limited knowledge skews the holy Scripture to match our own interpretations. Without God's laws, who knows what kind of people we would be? God's law are a testament to God's nature, the requirements to live in harmony with Him and with each other. Today you can see what a society looks like without God.

God wants all of us—and I mean *all of us*—to adopt it; He does not want to lose anyone to hell. The Ten Commandments are rules, laws, and decrees that teach us how to live our lives in ways that are pleasing to God. They also tell us how we are to act toward our neighbor and our fellow Christian. These acts were holy then, they are holy now, and they will always be holy in the future. God is the same today as He always has been and ever will be.

Christ's birth and death on the cross did not change the Torah or any of God's written law. Rather, His birth, death, and resurrection have fulfilled the laws.[7] The Jews of the time accused Jesus of blasphemy because He said plainly that He was God. They could not see that he was the Messiah they had been waiting centuries for because they were blinded by power and corruption. Possibly, God himself kept them from knowing so His will and plan would not fail. This stiff-necked people, as God proclaimed them, had inherited hundreds of years of standards that *they* had set, not God. They had a point of view and would not change it. No one could tell them how to interpret the Torah. Jesus stated that He had come to fulfill the law, not abolish it. He warned them about how far they had strayed from the intent of the law and the prophets. Because of this, they crucified Him.

After His death and resurrection, Jesus sent us the Holy Spirit to live in us and empower us to fulfill His commands. This happened at Pentecost. Now we are teamed up with Christ, who gives us the ability to live and pray to God because He became our intercessor, our high priest, in the order of Melchizedek.[8] We can pray directly to God through Christ with our petitions because of Christ's death and resurrection. We also now have the ability to live holy lives through the power of the Holy Spirit living in us.[9]

When Jesus was teaching His disciples, He used parables and storytelling to communicate His lessons. In doing so, He commissioned the New Testament that left instructions for Christians to follow. He gave us the correct response to our fallen nature: holy living. These same words have been used throughout history: *repent and be baptized.* Fall on your knees and return to Jesus. Jesus summed up all the Laws and Commands into two Commandments, which were called the Royal Commands by the Hebrews.

---

7 Matthew 5:17
8 Hebrews 7:11
9 Romans 6

In Deuteronomy 6:4-5, Moses reiterates the First Commandment to the nation of Israel:

> *"Hear, O Israel: The LORD our God, the LORD is One. And you shall love the LORD your God with all your heart and with all your soul and with all your strength."*

And in Leviticus 19:18, the Lord spoke unto Moses:

> *"You shall not take vengeance or bear a grudge against any of your people, but you shall love your neighbor as yourself: I am the LORD."*

Over 1,500 years had passed between the conquest of the Promised Land and the time of Jesus. At some point during that time, Israel adopted these two commands as Royal Commands. Having converted followers by the thousands with His miracles and healings, Jesus was upsetting the Jewish rulers' power structure. One day, the Jewish rulers attempted to trap Jesus into saying something that would be contrary to their interpretation of the Mosaic law so they could arrest Him. The Sanhedrin sent an expert in the law, a Pharisee, who was full of pride and planned to test him on the Royal Commands. Matthew 22:36-40 recounts the story of the Pharisees and the trap they laid for Jesus:

> *"Teacher, which is the greatest commandment in the law?"*
> *Jesus replied: "'Love the Lord your God with all your heart and with all your soul and with all your mind.' This is the First and greatest commandment. And the second is like it: 'Love your neighbor as yourself.* ***All the Law and the Prophets hang on these two commandments.'"***

I want everyone to read and reread Jesus's final statement. Read it again, again, and again. Ponder on it and pray about it and ask for wisdom. What does this mean? *All the Law and all the Prophets hang on these two commandments.* This says it all. Jesus not only knew the Royal Commandments precisely—He defined them. I don't see any other way to interpret this! Jesus summed up all the laws and prophets into two Royal Commands.

Israel interpreted it this same way, but they still had to complete and practice all the other 400-plus laws under the rulers at that time. I have no written proof here, but I think the Pharisees were seeing if Jesus knew the two Royal Commandments to test His knowledge. What they failed to realize was that He *wrote* the law, that He *is* the law. It was passed from God's mouth to Moses, then to the Hebrews, then to us in the form of what we call the Bible. Who is Jesus? Was He not the word God spoke?[10] Was He not present when all things were made? Is He not also the Messiah? Yes, He is. Why did He come from heaven to earth? To save us from our sins. Not to condemn us, but to give us a way to God's salvation and eternal life. He wants to make this as simple as possible, your relationship with Him, that is.

I want to add some clarity to our lives here on this earth. What is our *purpose* in life? People are always searching for different ways in which to ease their souls and find their purpose in their lives. They miss the boat when they do not look to the creator of all things, seen and unseen. All of humanity was designed to glorify God. Let me repeat: **our purpose in life is to glorify God**. He who breathed the breath of life into us through Adam deserves our worship of Him. If we believe and acknowledge this fact, then we now have a mission in life. That mission is to live according to His commandments and share the Gospel with anyone and everyone. In John 14:15, He states the following:

> *"If you love Me, you will keep My commandments."*

---

10 John 1:1-3; Colossians 2:9

The Four Commandments of Christ™

ושי לש תודוקפה עברא

The Four Commands of Christ are Jesus's summation of the Ten Commandments, the Mosaic Law, and the Prophets. He added Two more Commandments in the New Testament.

First Command: *"Love the Lord your God with all your heart, and with all your soul, and with all your mind... This is the first and greatest commandment."* (Matthew 22:37-38) A person asked me, "What does this look like? I don't know how to do this." I asked Jesus for help, and He revealed this to me:
"Humble Yourself and Submit."

Second Command: *"And the second is like it, 'love your neighbor as yourself.' All the Law and the Prophets hang on these two commandments."* (Matthew 22:39-40) This command is the following:
"Give Grace and Mercy."

Third Command: *"A new command I give you: Love one another. As I have loved you, so you must love one another. By this everyone will know that you are my disciples, if you love one another."* (John 13:34-35) This command is the following:
"Practice Forgiveness within Your Church."

Fourth Command: *"Therefore, go and make disciples of all nations, baptizing them in the name of the Father and of the Son and of the Holy Spirit, and teaching them to obey everything I have commanded you. And surely I am with you always, to the very end of the age."* (Matthew 28:19-20) This command is the following:
"Your Mission in Life."

Spiritual Disciplines
These are spiritual disciplines that aid in developing strong roots as a Christian and fulfilling the Four Commands of Christ:

- *Know you are eternal*: You—your soul—will never die. Our souls cannot be created or destroyed. They are given to us at birth from God. We are eternal because God is eternal. God says He puts before us life and death; choose life. (Genesis 2:7, Deuteronomy 30:19)

- If Christ is not in your heart, then the first order of business is to **commit to Jesus** and accept Jesus into your heart. This brings life everlasting. (Acts 3:19, John 3:16, Revelation 3:20, Romans 10:9)

- *Get on your knees and pray.* Develop a prayer life. Praying is the cry of your heart, an expression of the First Command of Christ. (Psalm 10:17, Psalm 95:6, Romans 14:11, Daniel 6:10, Ephesians 3:14, Philippians 4:6, James 5:16, Psalm 34:15)

- *Read your Bible* every morning before you go to work and every night before you go to bed. (Deuteronomy 6:4-9)

- *Memorize Scripture.* After you have memorized the Four Commands, move on to other Scripture: John 3:16, John 9:4, John 14:15, Romans 6, and Romans 10:9 are good passages to start with.

- *Tithe your money*: 10 percent to God, 10 percent in savings, then live on the rest. (Malachi 3:8-10, Genesis 28:22, Nehemiah 10:38)

- *Tithe your time*: Dedicate time to the Lord. Start with ten minutes and work your way up. Mix it up with reading the Bible, memorization, fasting, Christian music, and read biographies about saints. (James 4: 8, Joshua 1:9, Psalm 1:2, Governing Values)

- ***Thank God always,*** for everything in your life on a constant basis. Thank Him all day long for everything, be it big or small. (1Timothy 4:4-5, 1Chronicles 16:34, Psalm 107:8-9)

- ***Practice fasting.*** Develop a fasting program, especially if you want God to answer certain prayer requests you may have. (Acts 13:2, Acts 14:23, Daniel 10:3, Esther 4:16, Joel 2:12)

Always remember straight and narrow is the Christian walk. What does this mean? ***Be disciplined***. You must have a paradigm change in your life and develop governing values and set priorities to overcome the world. "'But take heart,' Jesus says, 'I have overcome the world'" (Matthew 7:13-14, John 16:33). In Exodus 18:20, Moses was told to write this down concerning the Ten Commandments: *"Teach them His decrees and instructions, and show them the way they are to live and how they are to behave."* His decrees are the Four Commands of Christ. His instructions are listed just below each Command: humble yourself and submit, give grace and mercy, practice forgiveness, and live your mission. *Show them the way they are to live* is in the spiritual disciplines, and *how they are to behave* is in the whole Bible. The Four Commands of Christ fulfill all the requirements of the Old Testament as well as the New Testament.

It is our duty to overcome the world with the knowledge, perseverance, and faith with the testimony of Jesus Christ in our lives by practicing the Four Commands of Christ and the spiritual disciplines listed herein. We must work on the First Commands of Christ in order to reach our fullest capabilities in Christ. We need to make God our number-one governing value. What does that mean? When you spend your money, time, energy, and effort into yourself, make sure God gets the first fruit of that money, time, energy, and effort. I call this being in the zone. Then you are able to go and reach others for Christ and fill up the ark (church) because the time is short. We are living in the End Times, and birth pains are evident everywhere as stated in Matthew 24:8. Live your life as Christ commands and call your neighbor unto Jesus.

PART ONE

The Four Commands of Christ

Chapter One

First Command: Humble Yourself and Submit

"Love the Lord your God with all your heart and with all your soul and with all your mind. This is the first and greatest commandment."

Matthew 22:37-38

This First Command is Christ's summation of the first four commandments of the Ten Commandments: *"And thou shalt love the LORD thy God with all thine heart, and with all thy soul, and with all thy might"* (Deuteronomy 6:5). Moses used this language to remind Israel before they entered the Promised Land to never forget who freed them, saved them, and guided them to a Promise made to Abraham.

I recently wrote to a pastor in Nebraska to share my vision of the Four Commands of Christ. In his reply, he asked me, "What does that mean, to love the Lord your God with all your heart and with all your soul and with all your mind?" He said he didn't know what it looked like and was deeply concerned that it had eluded him. In preparing my own response, I also struggled to express a definitive answer. What is the definition of this command? I stretched my mind as far as it would go, yet I could not come up with an answer that was sufficient.

Six months later, the Holy Spirit opened my mind to how we can accomplish each of the commands. He gave me the instructions to complete each command and adopt them into our lives. For the First Command of Christ, God gave me this to adopt into our spiritual walk. We are to ***humble ourselves and submit***.

This is it. It's so simple yet so hard to do, especially when we try to actively practice it. I was overjoyed that I could write back to the pastor in Nebraska and share this revelation. It was astounding how short, simple, and direct this was. Now my pursuit was to find out why we need to humble ourselves and how we are to submit!

Let's start with stories in the Bible of individuals who humbled themselves before the Lord:

- **Jesus,** The Son of God, was tried and convicted of sedition despite being falsely accused. He was whipped with a flagrum, spat upon, and finally nailed to the cross with a crown of thorns forced upon His head, yet not one of His bones was broken.[11] A spear was driven into His side to make sure He was dead before removing Him from the cross.[12] Yet, despite all the power He could have used, He still did not fight back. Humbly, He gave His life on that cross, a sacrificial lamb for you and me. He took our sins upon Himself so we could in Him be saved from eternal death.[13] Jesus Christ was the humblest of all men on earth ever, giving His life for us. This is especially amazing when we consider that He is God.

- **Job** lost all of his children and everything he owned and was plagued with boils, yet he humbled himself before God's questions. He did not turn his back on God as his wife had told him he should. His words are a testament to the depth of our spirit: *"Though he slay me, yet will I hope in him"* (Job 13:15).

11 Psalm 34:20
12 John 19:34
13 Luke 23:1-18

- **King David** humbled himself before the Lord. *"David's greatness was not in his bravery, even though he was very brave. It was not in the battles that he won, even though he won many. It was not in the glory of his reign, even though he had his share of glory. It was in his willingness to submit to the will of God and to humble his heart in repentance when he sinned."* [14]

- **Ruth** took care of her mother-in-law after her husband died and then humbly laid at the feet of Boaz so that she could become his wife and support her mother-in-law. This is a great story about redemption from the Old Testament and a foreshadowing of what was to come with Christ on the cross. [15]

- **Mary Magdalene** humbly wept at Jesus's feet, washing them with her tears and drying them with her hair. [16]

- **Peter** died for his beliefs. It has been told that he asked to be crucified upside down because he said he was not worthy to be crucified in the same way as Jesus.

- **Paul**, once known as Saul, was blinded by God on the road to Damascus. Though he had worked to stifle and defeat Christians, he humbly asked a Christian to heal him from blindness. [17]

- **Moses** was a prince of Egypt and a leader in the Egyptian military, yet he humbled himself by following God's instructions, relying on God's judgment rather than his own, and allowing others to rule with him. Perhaps tending sheep for forty years taught Moses an important lesson in humility. *"Now Moses was a very humble man, more humble than anyone else on the face of the earth"* (Numbers 12:3).

---

14 http://www.christianlibrary.org/authors/Grady_Scott/david2.htm
15 Ruth 3
16 John 12:3
17 Acts 9

Each humbling act by these saints speaks to each of us. These examples of humility highlight God's love for us when we are humble and help us to understand how we should respond to God's direction for our lives.

We need to learn how the act of "humbling ourselves before God" will draw us into a closer relationship with Him and override our desire to follow our own path. David shows us a good example of what it means to be humbled before the Lord by teaching us to seek God through constant prayer in the name of Jesus. Maybe a definition of "to be humble before the Lord" is to admit you are wrong in anything and everything you do that is contrary to God's wish and design for your life.[18] Continuously ask God to remove the beam from your eye.[19]

Acknowledge Him in all your ways. (Proverbs 3:3-9)

If my people, who are called by my name, will humble themselves and pray and seek my face and turn from their wicked ways, then I will hear from heaven, and I will forgive their sin and will heal their land. Now my eyes will be open and my ears attentive to the prayers offered in this place. (2 Chronicles 7:14)

These Scriptures help us to understand what being humble and submitting to God's will looks like, and I encourage you to explore the Bible and find passages that speak to you. There are many more passages to deepen our understanding even further, including the following:

- 1 Peter 5:5
- Job 22:21
- Matthew 18:4
- Matthew 23:12

---

18 Zachariah 12
19 Matthew 7

- James 4:6
- James 4:10
- Isaiah 66:2
- Psalms 138:16
- Proverbs 3:34
- Proverbs 11:12
- Proverbs 15:35
- Proverbs 18:12
- Proverbs 29:23

To humble yourself and submit puts you in a place where God's love covers you completely and keeps you **in the zone**. But submitting to God can be difficult to figure out! Satan seems to steal away the plan God has for us when we do not focus on Him daily. Satan takes us away from our mission by reminding us of our past sins, past hurts, and past unresolved issues that prevent us from having a clear conscience. Sometimes we have sin hidden away in our heart and will not walk away from it. For that reason, we don't—and can't—move into a closer relationship with God. We need to learn how to submit to God's will so we can come out of that relation with clean hands and a pure heart and can work on the mission God has given us.

Maybe we can't let go of a temptation or an emotion that continues to haunt us. God has likely been quietly telling us to remove this or that from our lives, and we just say "no" or, "I will tomorrow." The Book of James teaches us about how to understand what temptation is.

> *When tempted, no one should say, "God is tempting me." For God cannot be tempted by evil, nor does he tempt anyone; but each person is tempted when they are dragged away by their own evil desire and enticed. Then, after desire has conceived, it gives birth to sin; and sin, when it is full-grown, gives birth to death. (James 1:13-15)*

Maybe another reason we cave into temptation is that we don't submit to Christ and use Christ's teaching to do as we were instructed: *"Deny yourself and take up your cross and follow me, daily"* (Luke 9:23). Maybe we no longer think of walking with Christ as something to be cherished and instead put our wishes before Christ's. Some of us may worry that, if we submit to Christ, then we will be restricted from habits that we don't want to give up. Some don't always humble themselves enough to listen to God, even when they know they should.

So, what exactly does it mean to submit? **Submitting** means putting others before yourself. It means not always doing what you want to do. It means putting God's desires above your desires. It means to *surrender*. When we submit ourselves, we surrender ourselves to Christ as He surrendered Himself to God on the cross. When we bow our heads in prayer, is this not submitting or surrendering our will to God's?

I find it difficult to understand why our nature is such that, even with Christ in our hearts and a deep love for the triune God, we still fail. And I am disappointed that sin nature had such a powerful hold on my psyche before I learned to humble myself and submit. Now, I know what a lot of you will say: it's just how we are, and we can't change our nature. This mindset corrupts our relationship with Christ. I am not willing to accept this mindset. Are you?

> *What shall we say then? Shall we continue in sin, that grace may abound? (Romans 6:1 KJV)*

> *So, my brothers and sisters, you also died to the law through the body of Christ, that you might belong to another, to him who was raised from the dead, in order that we might bear fruit for God. For when we were in the realm of the flesh, the sinful passions aroused by the law were at work in us, so that we bore fruit for death. But now, by dying to what once bound us, we have been released from the law so that we serve in the new way of the Spirit, and not in the old way of the written code. (Romans 7:4-6)*

*What a wretched man I am! Who will rescue me from this
body of death? Thanks be to God, through Jesus Christ our
Lord. (Romans 7:24-25)*

In these passages, Paul described the struggle that we have within
ourselves: trying to rectify our fallen nature with that of the new nature
that Jesus gave us when we accepted Him as our Savior. We need to
learn to submit our entire self to God every morning and night in order
to overcome our fallen nature. This requires us to reset our habits and
develop new governing values.

Solomon exemplifies how, despite this struggle, we can humble
ourselves and surrender to God. When Solomon became king, God told
Solomon to ask for anything, and He would give it to him. Solomon
humbled himself before the Lord and did not ask for riches, long life,
or power; instead, he asked for wisdom to rule over God's people.
Because of that request, God gave him riches and glory in addition to
knowledge to rule God's people, Israel. Though Solomon used these
gifts to accomplish great things, such as building the First Temple in
Jerusalem, those gifts soon corrupted his soul. He caved to his manly
desires, one of which was to have many wives, and gave in to worshiping
their own gods. He did exactly what God told the Nation of Israel not
to do: marry the women of the foreigners that God was removing from
the Promised Land. God knew that marrying women outside of Israel
would bring false gods into their lives and corrupt them. The good news
is that by the end of his life, he finally realized his faults. He repented
in the face of what he had become and his past.

*When all has been heard, the conclusion of the matter is
this: Fear God and keep His commandments, because this is
the whole duty of man. For God will bring every deed into
judgment, along with every hidden thing, whether good or
evil. (Ecclesiastes 12:13-14)*

This is why Christ says to all of us:

Take up your cross and follow me.[20]

You still lack one thing. Sell everything you have and give to the poor, and you will have treasure in heaven. Then come, follow me.[21]

You cannot serve two masters.[22]

I am the way, the truth and the life.[23]

You can continue exploring these themes in the following passages:

- Romans 6
- Matthew 26:39
- Matthew 14:36
- Galatians 5:24
- 1 John 3:4
- Colossians 3:5
- Acts 17:30
- James 4:7
- Job 22:21
- Hebrews 10:5-7
- Hebrews 13:17
- Revelations 2:7

* * * * * * *

---

20 Matthew 16:24b paraphrased by the author
21 Luke 18:22 paraphrased by author
22 Matthew 6:24a paraphrased by author
23 John 14:6

In my own life, I have experienced profound healing through humbling myself and submitting to God. I always knew God was sovereign, but I did not truly understand what it looked like until it showed up at my front door.

Recently, I was diagnosed with prostate cancer. God had revealed to me about ten years ago that I would die from cancer, but He did not tell me when. I am not sure why He told me, but I do know Jesus has talked about the subject of death with His disciples. For all of these years, I have been wondering when I would die from cancer, and, to be honest, I thought that I had three or four more years left.

Well, the day finally came, and it arrived earlier than I expected. Cancer was confirmed with 95 percent at stage 4 and 5 percent at stage 5. Needless to say, this was not great news. I figured this was it for me not only because of my age and my family history (I am almost seventy years old, and most of my relatives died from cancer) but also because of what God had revealed to me almost a decade ago.

The emotional and mental battle you go through when you are told you have cancer is hard to describe. I went through a litany of wants and wishes for what I have not accomplished in my life yet. My grandchildren are young, and I want to watch them grow up. I want to be a part of their physical and spiritual growth. I want to spoil them and then send them home to their parents to deal with the consequences of my spoiling them. I don't want to leave my wife a widow. I'm not finished writing the book!

I thought of all the times I could have been writing and did not. I experienced guilt and sorrow and all the emotions a man can have when he doesn't know if he is going to live or die. I got on my knees and begged God for forgiveness for not being a better parent, a better husband, a better Christian. I begged for ten more years to spend time with my family, finish the book, start the projects I had planned, and preach. I prayed and prayed, and sorrow poured out of my soul. I believe God was listening to the cry of my heart. I hadn't received any definitive answers, but I felt peaceful and secure about my future. Maybe the operative phrase is *shalom Adonai*.

I was supposed to have radiation treatment that week because my urologist determined I was not fit for prostatectomy surgery. After the doctor explained the procedure and what would happen to my body, I went home feeling so discouraged. During my prayer time the next day, I felt impressed by the Holy Spirit to go to another hospital to see about having a prostatectomy instead of radiation treatment. I felt God leading me in this direction. After consulting with the other hospital's urology department, I was told that I barely qualified for this operation, but they would do it. Praise the Lord! This was an answer to my prayer. I was hoping God would just heal me, but could this removal of the prostate gland be the way He was going to heal me?

I started praying that God would take away the cancer so I wouldn't have to go through radiation or any other postoperative procedures. I continued in prayer. Then, one morning, God came to me in my prayer time and impressed on me that I would be healed from cancer, and He would also extend my life for ten more years. I was so happy. I was dancing around with joy and told my wife what God shared with me in my prayer. The next day, my pastor and an associate pastor came to pray over me and anoint me with oil. I felt like telling them that God already had this, but I submitted and was very happy for it. God works in mysterious ways. I was so confident in my prayer and in what I thought God had said to me that I told everyone God was going to heal me from this cancer.

As I lay in the hospital bed recovering from the surgery, the doctor came to my room to tell me the operation went perfectly and that they got all the cancer out. In fact, I wouldn't need any radiation or chemo. I was so happy. I knew this would happen, though, because God had told me in my prayer that I would be healed. So, I went around saying I was free of cancer. I was very sure of what God had done, and in my soul, I felt Him assuring me. Two months later, I was back in the hospital for a follow-up appointment. After running a few tests, they told me that not all of the cancer had been removed. The doctor asked me to come back in four weeks.

I was devastated. I almost broke down right there in front of the doctor, thinking, "God, you said!" I hid the battle going on inside of me because I didn't want the doctor to see it. I couldn't believe that I wasn't healed. I was mad at God. I began to wonder if anything in my life was true because I had been so sure that he would heal me. I struggled for the next few days and tried to figure out what I had done wrong to cause this outcome. Why had He told me I was healed or allowed me to misunderstand what I thought He had said to me in prayer? God was silent.

In James, he says, *"When you doubt, you are like the ocean waves in a storm"* (James 1:6). Satan was winning the battle of doubt that I harbored in my mind. I will admit that God and I were estranged during that time. Finally, I stopped blaming God for my struggle and started questioning myself. After much more prayer, I finally came to a conclusion: even if God doesn't talk to me anymore because of my doubt, I will worship Him and continue to walk in His ways. These thoughts went through my mind:

I am the clay. He is the Potter.[24]

He decides if I am made for noble or ignoble purpose, not me.

I live or die in service to Him.

Though He slay me, yet will I serve Him.

Not my will but Thine.

I humble myself before you, Lord, and submit.

You are my God. Where else would I go?

There is nothing else out there and no one else to turn to except my Maker.

---

24 Isaiah 64:8

I have to admit that accepting these teachings from the Bible brought peace to my soul. God used the Bible and the words I stored up in my heart to teach me how to behave. I was able to move on with my life, even though I still did not totally understand. I just trusted in what I knew of God's nature. Here again: *shalom Adonai.*

I endured some time without really knowing if God was present in my life. He was not answering me or filling me with the Holy Spirit in the same manner as he had before my doubt. I am not saying God was not with me. Rather, I am saying that I couldn't feel Him in my heart like I used to. I was so accustomed to a relationship of communication between us that when He was quiet, I grew nervous. When you are in the zone, you get used to the daily communion and interaction with God. You know you are in His presence. This feeling of leanness was worse than knowing I wasn't healed of cancer! At the time, I did not know what to expect. Should I look to my interpretation of what I thought God was telling me, or would I run the risk of misunderstanding God again?

For a time, I was unsure what I should adopt as communication between myself and God. My outlook was not positive, and I was unsure of myself and struggling with my interpretation of what I thought was truth. I held on to this one truth, however: Whether I live or I die, I will trust in Jesus. Paul wrote in Romans 14:8, *"If we live, we live for the Lord; and if we die, we die for the Lord. So, whether we live or die, we belong to the Lord."*

One month later, I was back in the doctor's office with another checkup. My test results had not improved. So, I figured I was toast, and it was only a short time before I'd be seeing Jesus. However, the doctor informed me that with hormone and radiation treatment, they were seeing a 10- to 15-year extension on people's lives with cancer like mine. I thought to myself, "Ten more years, isn't that what God promised me?" Even though it wasn't exactly what I had expected, I could accept that. I thanked Jesus under my breath and asked Him to forgive me for my doubt. The doctor told me to come back in a week for a PET scan that would determine where the cancer had spread.

This morning, before heading out to my PET scan, I saw an email from my memorization program that I subscribe to.[25] The message was unbelievable:

"Just as Moses lifted up the snake in the wilderness, so the
Son of Man must be lifted up, that everyone who believes
may have eternal life in him." (John 3:14-15)

In comparing the snake on a bronze pole to Himself, Jesus prophesized to Nicodemus what was going to happen to Him and how beneficial it would be to the world for Him to die on the cross. The snake on the pole and Jesus on the cross are both forces of healing, and both instances require faith. Jesus's death on the cross heals if we believe in Him. Jesus obliterates our sins; there is no more to be seen by Him because we are covered with His blood.

For me, the most important part of this story is that God gave Moses a remedy for Israel's snakebite that was killing them; if they were bitten by a snake and by faith looked at the snake on the bronze pole, they were healed. Similarly, God has given us Jesus as a remedy for our healing and gift of eternal life. If you do not look to Jesus for your salvation, you will die in your sin to eternal death. In the same way that God did not remove the snakes from among them, God has not removed sin from this World yet. If we believe in Jesus and ask for forgiveness, He will heal us. Jesus said to me that my cancer is still here, but because I have faith in Him, I am healed. Will I live another ten years? Yes, I will, only because my life is His. I love Him with ALL my heart, all my soul, and all my mind, every cubic inch of me.

If we humble ourselves and submit and accept the truth that it is up to God how we are healed, then we will not have the disappointments so many experience. I misunderstood God's plan for my life with cancer and the lessons He wanted me to learn from it. Believe me, He has nothing but my and your best interests at heart. It is always up to God how He uses us for His glory. This is why we were born: *to*

---

25 Institute in Basic Life Principles

glorify God. This is our purpose in life. We are His clay to shape and mold as He wishes. If my cancer can glorify God, Amen. Better yet, if this journey has made me a better man, Amen. He is sculpting me to understand God better so I can then help others in their journey with Christ. I still have cancer, but I have the Holy Spirit who is my high tower and keeps the deadliness of cancer at bay. It can do nothing to me unless God allows it to. Praise God.

* * * * * * *

We must follow His commandments, and He has broken them down into only four commands that sum up all the others. Practice the Four Commands of Christ. Below are some examples of what Jesus taught in terms of how to follow Him:

> *In fact, this is love for God: to keep his commands. And his commands are not burdensome. (1 John 5:3)*

> *If you love me, keep my commands. (John 14:15)*

> *Whoever has my commands and keeps them is the one who loves me. The one who loves me will be loved by my Father, and I too will love them and show myself to them. (John 14:21)*

This should help you to submit daily because you know how important it is to God. It is **life** for us.

- One expression of submission you can do is to kneel first thing every morning before God in prayer.

- Give your neighbor Grace and Mercy (second command). Don't condemn them for the splinter in their eye when you still have a beam in yours. (Luke 6:36, Hebrews 4:16, Matthew 7:3-5)

- Make sure if you have conflict with your brother in the church, you have forgiven him and ask for forgiveness from him (third Command of Christ). (Colossians 3:13, Matthew 6:14-15, Matthew 18:21, Luke 17:3-4)

- Develop a prayer life. Prayer is the cry of your heart. Figure out what works for you and develop a plan for daily prayer. Don't let the business of life rob you of this time. (Philippians 4:6, James 5:16, Psalm 34:15)

Always be ready to share Jesus with anyone, anytime, and anywhere. Share what Jesus has done in your life and how He has blessed you. Ask if they would like to personally know Jesus. Use the Four Commands of Christ as your basis. (Fourth Command; Matthew 28:19)

Chapter Two

Second Command: Give Grace and Mercy

"And the second is like it: 'Love your neighbor as yourself.' All the Law and the Prophets hang on these two commandments."

Matthew 22:39-40

God summed all the commandments, prophecies, and laws into the two Royal Commandments. When I asked God to reveal how we can adopt the first Royal Commandment to love God with all of our heart, soul, and mind, he showed me the answer: to humble ourselves and submit. In this second Royal Commandment, we are asked to love our neighbors. What does it mean to love your neighbor as yourself? How do we apply this Royal Commandment to our own lives? How do I love my neighbor when I don't even love myself? Here is Jesus's answer to this question: give grace and mercy. God gave us grace and mercy when He forgave us; He expects us to do the same for our neighbor.

But what does giving grace mean? Differences in Bible translations reveal interesting interpretations of the word "grace." Let's compare passages from the King James and New International versions:

	KJV	**NIV**
Genesis 6:8	*"but Noah found* **grace** *in the eyes of the Lord"*	*"but Noah found* **favor** *in the eyes of the Lord"*
Genesis 47:29	*"if now I have found* **grace** *in thy sight"*	*"If I have found* **favor** *in your eyes"*

We can see that "grace" in the King James translation has been replaced with "favor" in the New International translation. In the New Testament, however, the Greek word for *grace* is *Charis*; both interpretations would seem to be interchangeable. Thus, when we give grace to our neighbor, it means we give him favor. Rather than holding a grudge or hatred toward our neighbor, we give them the favor of our heart, mind, soul and strength. We love them as God loves us.

Everyone wants grace, especially grace from God. All of us want to be forgiven for the sins we have committed against God, against humanity, and sometimes against ourselves. When we ask Christ into our hearts, God extends grace to us, through Christ, from the wrath that we deserve. The blood of Jesus Christ covers our sins and allows us to receive this grace. Because we have received grace from Christ, He expects us to extend grace to our neighbor. Jesus is asking us to forgive them immediately, even as they are sinning against us.

Whether people are Christians or not, everyone wants to receive the favor of others, to be given grace. We notice others' actions and how they treat us. If we as Christians practice this command, people will notice that there is something different about us. If your brother offends you, do not return evil for evil, but give your neighbor grace and mercy.[26] Then pray that God will change your heart toward them or maybe theirs toward you. After all, we carry the beam in our own eye, do we not?[27] Whatever the issue is, learn to put it on the altar and

---

26 Matthew 5:38-47
27 Matthew 7:5

let God fight the battle for you. You must return good for evil, turn the other cheek, walk a mile with your neighbor, be the good Samaritan.[28] When we put all these Scriptures together, we start to see what Christ meant when he commanded us to love your neighbor as yourself.

* * * * * * *

Mercy is one of God's virtues that is so wonderful that no words or images would ever be a suitable description. Because God is so holy, mercy is a natural outpouring of His love toward us, His creation. God's mercy flows out of Him, even though His creation seems to turn their backs on Him. His mercy is also always there for humanity to accept. God's mercy toward humanity is such that He sent His only begotten Son to the cross to redeem us.[29] His mercy falls on all of us at one point and time in our lives. His mercy calls us to Him; it is only our hardened hearts that separate us from that mercy. Could we say that Jesus is God's mercy toward humanity?

God's mercy is always working for us.[30] For instance, take His promise to Abraham that all peoples on earth will be blessed through him.[31] Israel came out of Abraham, and throughout their history, God has blessed them. When the nation of Israel sins and is taken into captivity by political powers, and removed from the Promised Land, He always saves a remnant and brings them back to their homeland. He blesses them with productivity and security until they sin again. Even when in captivity or scattered in different nations, God is still with them. He honors them with Himself even though they don't deserve it. It is all because of His promise. His love and mercy never fails even though Israel does not recognize Jesus as their Messiah. His mercy is still on them. His protection, His healing of the land, is evident. If you were to fly over Israel now, you would see how their land has been turned into a garden, the land of milk and honey. Just as God's grace and mercy

28 Luke 10:30-36
29 John 3:16
30 Romans 8:28
31 Genesis 22:18

toward Israel will never be revoked, God will always extend His mercy toward us whether we accept it or not. Please remember this, Jesus came to save, not to condemn.[32]

Why should we worry about the promise God made to Abraham? God's mercy is always working to bring all peoples into fellowship with Him, just as He has done for Israel. Throughout the Old Testament, God showed Israel mercy. Even in captivity, God gave them mercy and protected them as He does for Christians. The Book of Esther tells how God intervened on behalf of the Jewish nation to keep them from being annihilated.[33] Daniel prayed three times a day, and when he was thrown in the lion's den because of his prayer life,[34] God intervened with His mercy, shutting the mouths of the lions. During that same time, Shadrach, Meshach, and Abednego were also steadfast in following God's laws and prayed to Him daily. When faced with a fiery death as punishment for refusing to bow to the king's image, God showed them mercy. They not only survived the fire but also walked through the fire with Jesus.[35] He was probably telling them about the coming of the Four Commands of Christ.

God's mercy on all of us is evident in our stories of what might have been. If we were able to collect all the stories of the missed disasters that God saved us from, what a book that would be. I was once involved in an accident, and had I not put my seatbelt on, I would have probably been a vegetable the rest of my life. Because I submitted when God told me to put my seatbelt on, I am alive. People fail to give God credit where credit is due for all the near misses we have gone through.

God shows the virtues of grace and mercy in Exodus. While Moses was receiving the Ten Commandments on the mountaintop, the people of Israel forced Aaron to make a golden calf and began to worship the idol. God told Moses that He was going to destroy the nation of Israel for their sins. Moses pleaded with God to punish him also. In the end, God told Moses to lead His people to the Promised Land. Before Moses

32 John 3:17
33 Ester 8 and 9
34 Daniel 6:10-24
35 Daniel 3:8-30

and Israel left for the Promised Land, Moses asked God a question. He wanted to make sure that his relationship with God was not in jeopardy and that God would still go with him. God gave Moses some assurance by showing Moses His back side, as no one had seen God's face and lived. God said to Moses as He passed by:

> And the LORD said, *"I will cause all my goodness to pass in front of you, and I will proclaim my name, the LORD, in your presence. **I will have mercy on whom I will have mercy**, and I will have compassion on whom I will have compassion." (Exodus 33:19)*

This statement was meant not only for Moses and Israel but also for us today. I believe that God has extended His mercy to the world knowing that the end will soon come. God does not desire anyone to be lost but will always call men unto Himself through Christ to be saved until the rapture. He does not want anyone to be separated from Him for eternity. He wants all of us to join Him in heaven and have eternal life, not eternal death. Don't harden your heart when God extends His grace or mercy to you. Accept it with a humility and cry out in thanks.

God is the same today and tomorrow. He has never changed. God is pure and holy, and most people have known this throughout the ages. A scene from William Shakespeare's *The Merchant of Venice* captures how we are closer to God when we practice mercy.

> *The quality of mercy is not strain'd.*
>
> *It droppeth as the gentle rain from heaven*
>
> *Upon the place beneath. It is twice blest:*
>
> *It blesseth him that gives, and him that takes.*

'Tis mightiest in the mightiest; it becomes

The throned monarch better than his crown.

His scepter shows the force of temporal power,

The attribute to awe and majesty,

Wherein doth sit the dread and fear of kings;

But mercy is above this sceptered sway;

It is enthroned in the hearts of kings;

It is an attribute to God himself;

And earthly power doth then show likest God's

When mercy seasons justice.[36]

* * * * * * *

Develop a prayer life that will lead to a deep love for Christ. He says in 2 Chronicles 7:14, *"If my people, who are called by my name, will humble themselves and pray and seek my face and turn from their wicked ways, then I will hear from heaven, and I will forgive their sin and will heal their land."* Another way to read this could be to insert your personal life for the corporate intent here by replacing "land" with "mind, body, and soul." Amen. By giving your neighbor mercy, you will receive mercy. If you forgive your neighbor, God will forgive you. We should always carry the mindset to give our neighbors grace and mercy.

36 *Shakespeare, William, 1564-1616. The Merchant of Venice. Harlow, Essex, England: Longman, 1994.*

Chapter Three

Third Command: Practice Forgiveness within Your Church

"A new command I give you: Love one another. As I have loved you, so you must love one another. By this everyone will know that you are my disciples, if you love one another."

John 13:34-35

When the Holy Spirit had me pause over this Scripture, I kept saying to myself, "I don't really know what this means!" Why would we need a new commandment on love when He had already summed up the Ten Commandments into, "Love the Lord and love your neighbor," the two Royal Commands? I started with the foundational questions: when, where, what, why, and how? When and where were clear. Jesus and His disciples had just finished supper and were still in the upper room. He had told them that He would be gone soon and that they could not follow Him. Take note that, when He is expressing this new command to His disciples, Judas is not there.

Christ's statement seems to belong in another chapter. After all, His discussion with the disciples is about a future event, about how He will not be with them anymore and they cannot follow![37] And in the middle of all of this, Jesus states, *"A new command I give you, love one another. As I have loved you, love one another. By this, everyone will know that you are my disciples, if you love one another"* (John 13:34-35).

You would have thought that all the disciples would have asked, "What do you mean, 'love one another?'" Instead, Peter is more worried about where Jesus is going. I think, at the time, it flew right over their heads. I believe they all missed this point that Jesus brought up, and maybe you have too all these years. Love one another? Wow, what a statement… but do we get it yet? Who was Jesus talking with when He made that statement? What happened when Jesus was resurrected and He defeated death? Were not His disciples the beginning of a new Church on this Earth? I have concluded that this new command, to love one another, is for the *New Church* that Jesus just began. The life and death of Jesus and His teachings that He gave His disciples started a new era of religion mixed with the old. This New Church started with the eleven disciples (the twelfth disciple had not been chosen, yet, following Judas's death), with Peter being the rock, the base. The disciples were the beginning of the churches that would grow from their evangelism. Now, I know some of you will say, "What about Paul and Barnabas?" I agree, but even they sent their tithe and support to the apostles in Jerusalem.

By His death and resurrection, He gave humanity a way to inherit the Kingdom of God that has always been Israel's destiny. He became the ultimate sacrifice, never again having to rely on the Mosaic law of sacrifice for our sins. By asking Jesus for forgiveness of our sins and accepting Him into our hearts, we are born again.[38] Baptism is the anchor, just as the Earth was baptized with water during the time of Noah. The old corrupt nations of people on Earth at that time refused to repent. They were buried in the flood of water as judgement. Nothing on Earth was above the water—no land, no trees, and eventually no birds. Noah, his family, and the animals that were in the Ark were all that were saved by God. They emerged from the flood with a newness

---

37 John 13:31-36
38 John 3:3

of life as a family that loved God and new animals to populate the Earth. Let us all walk in newness of life also.

Accepting Christ as your Savior is the only way into heaven, and Jesus wanted Israel to accept this. He was their Messiah, foretold all through the Torah. Some of the Jews accepted that He was the Messiah, but most did not. At least some knew, the Pharisees, that they would be resurrected sometime after death, but none of them knew anything about being born again, being filled with the Holy Spirit, and walking a holy life with Jesus forever.[39] This took time for each convert to learn as they searched the Scriptures, much like converts today need time. Some of us are still figuring it out.

This command to love one another is not for your neighbor or your friend. It's not even for the Samaritan. It is for all of us brothers and sisters who belong to His church. Jesus enjoined His disciples to love one another as examples for the new converts that will be coming forth out of the apostles' missionary work. Jesus wanted all Christians to be known by their love for one another. He said, *"Then they will know you are my disciples"* (John 13:35). People want to be a part of loving one another, but it seems that this is a strange commodity anymore. The Scripture says to love your neighbor and your enemy. Can we say that sometimes, Scripture can have several interpretations based on what God wants to reveal to us at the time. Jesus uses Scripture and its unlimited depth to educate and encourage us as needs arise.

This new Command to love one another inside the walls of our churches and synagogues would seem to stand in contrast to the dictum of an eye for eye and a tooth for a tooth.[40] I have not heard anyone talk about this phrase "love one another" applied inside the church! He knew our hearts—past, present, and future—and wanted to make sure that we followed this new rule, The Third Command of Christ, which is to love one another. When you become members of Jesus Christ's church and you love one another, then they will know you are His followers. He did not want to leave this world without establishing a new rule for us Christians to follow.

---

39 Acts 19:2
40 Exodus 21:24

Jesus also knew there would be disagreements between us humans in starting His church here on Earth. The church started with converted Jews. Paul also took the gospel to the gentiles (anyone who wasn't a Jew).[41] Paul was our apostle commissioned by Christ to show us the way. Other churches were eventually formed out of his missionary work. You can see where this needed to be a new command. Even today, the modern church is guilty of not loving one another.

I once belonged to a church that pushed their pastor out because of the modern music he introduced to the services, which many people enjoyed. However, the older, more established parishioners wanted the traditional music, and they did not want any other music played. This disagreement about music went so far that one of the leaders of the church took our music pastor to lunch and asked him to resign, so that the pastor would get the message and leave. Where was the love that Christ asked us to have within the church walls? When I heard this, it affected me deeply. I could not support the church anymore, and I retreated into my cocoon. It took a long time for me to come out of it. I know I was thin-skinned and should have had a more mature response, but I didn't. Over time, I matured and can now stand in a stronger, more knowledgeable way. I owe it all to applying the Four Commands of Christ to my life.

In another incident when I was a younger Christian, I was on the board of a church in Northern California. We were discussing adding on an education wing at the church when two of the board members started arguing over issues that were twenty years old. I couldn't believe my ears! This was not a good witness to the congregation, who had heard about the issue at the board meeting. This same board forced the pastor out and made him retire, a man who was called by God at eight years old to preach and served Christ all his life. Where was the love? The board called a new pastor to the church but wanted a unanimous vote. I voted no because I could not in good conscience vote yes after having read his résumé. I prayed about it every day and did not get a yes from Jesus, either. I continued with my no vote. Finally, they

---

41 Romans 15:16

figured out who was voting no and went after me to vote yes. I finally gave in to their pressure and voted yes. Then I resigned and left the church. That church went from a church attendance of 400 people to 125 within three years. I often wondered what would have happened if I would have stuck to my convictions. Would I have been banished? Would I have been shunned? All I know is that we definitely did not practice love for one another.

How many of us are holding back love for a fellow Christian because we think they are stained? In your after-church conversations, have you heard other members relate to another member with a color that is not tasteful, commenting on someone's divorce or new spouse? These are the holier-than-thou types, the ones that shun others because of their past. I guess Christ's forgiveness is only for those who never had sin in their life. The problem with all this is our church temperament spreads throughout the community, and some people may make their mind up to never attend a church that talks in such a way about its members. Can't we forgive one another, especially those who have fallen away and returned? Christ forgave us; can't the Church forgive them, too? It seems to me Jesus said that if we don't forgive our brothers and sisters, He won't forgive us! Whoever is without sin should cast the first stone, and those of you who are sinless should throw the first one. Everyone lives in a glass house and has sinned. As it is written, *"There is none righteous, no, not one"* (Romans 3:10). So, be careful what you say about another brother or sister. We sometimes are our own worst enemy. We need to practice forgiveness and love one another inside our churches so the local community will want to come and be a part of our church. This is the operative word and action plan for this command: *forgiveness.*

* * * * * * *

After His resurrection, Jesus sat by the shore with a fire, waiting on the seven disciples who had gone fishing with Peter to return. After telling them to cast their net to the right side of the boat and filling their net with abundant fish, He waited for them to row back. When they arrived, Jesus said to the group, "Come and have breakfast." The risen Jesus cooked and ate fish and had bread with his disciples for the last time. He then turned to Peter after they were done eating and said, "Peter, follow me." Jesus was restoring Peter so he could start the New Church that He left in the disciples' hands. This encounter that Jesus had with Peter was intended to refocus him on his task as the "Rock" (not Dwayne Johnson).[42] He continued to tell Peter, "If you Love me, follow Me." He told him not to worry about other things, events, or people in your life. When Jesus restored Peter, He came into Peter's heart, soul, mind, and all his strength. Jesus reinstated Peter even after he denied Christ three times at the high priest's courtyard. Jesus will do the exact same thing for us. He comes into our hearts after we ask for forgiveness. "Follow Me," Jesus says to us.

The church is also being instructed with the same statements made to Peter. We are to follow Him and feed His sheep and not argue and fuss over disagreements within the church. Jesus said that, if we have a disagreement with our fellow man, we should leave our gift on the altar and fix it.[43] Jesus also tells us to get the beam out of our own eye before we work on the splinter in our neighbor's eye.[44] We must take every incident that bothers us to Jesus in prayer and ask Him to fix it before we have that meeting with our brother or sister. We also have to have the patience to wait for Jesus to work all things out for the best results. Use Psalm 51 for your prayer and work through your feelings. We need to put our desires and wishes on the altar and wait for his timing. Remember, let's practice forgiveness in all our interactions with our brothers and sisters in our churches. This is to the pastors: please preach forgiveness within the "corporate body" of your church so that the world will know we are Christ's disciples. This is a Commandment within our Church, to love one another so all outside our Church will know we are Christ's disciples.

We should practice love in our family and our extended family. Some recent statistics suggest that the divorce rate among Christians is equal to the non-Christian world. The family unit is falling apart and our society

---

42 Matthew 16:18
43 Matthew 5:23-24
44 Matthew 7:3

along with it. People do not realize how Christ's Commands are the fabric that holds us together as a people and a nation. Suicide rates, alcoholism, and drug use are all on the rise, and some states are approving all of this. They—our government—seem to be willing to let our most treasured asset—children and the family unit—fall to the wayside while they push wokeness nationally. They are allowing others with a reprobate mind to take the main stage, pushing all us Christians to accept or be pursued by weaponizing the government against us. I believe this is important to address because it is true and very harmful to us as a nation. Politics do and will play a part in the last days that we are in.

The government needs our prayers so they will know we are Christ's disciples. Pray that God will allow us to maintain our Christian nation status. Pray that our leaders will be turned toward the Light. If we don't love one another, we are all lost. If we don't get the First Command of Christ right, we will never get anything else right in our life. We must, must love the Lord our God with all our heart, mind, soul and strength. How do I keep my faith? I read my Bible. I pray. I fast. I tithe. I surrender. I humble myself and submit. I listen to great music and dance all around the living room floor, sometimes by myself and mostly with my wife and my grandchildren.

When my kids were young, we would listen to Christian children's music before church and dance. Christianity was fun for my kids. It was exciting to show them how to practice faith. Our house was always the home where the neighborhood kids would come and play. My wife was a stay-at-home mom, and she made sure that they all had fun every day. She provided an atmosphere of hospitality and excitement. One of those kids lived three houses up the street from us. His home environment was not good; his parents often stayed out partying all night. They always seemed to have an attitude against God and would not allow their child to attend Christian activities with us. We would include this kid in our daily children's activities around the house and outside, but he wasn't allowed to go to church with us.

One Sunday, my kids asked him to go to church with us. He said he would have to ask, but his parents would probably say no. My kids replied, "Well, tell them we are going somewhere else."

When I heard that, I said, "No. Here is how we are going to handle this."

Then I gathered them around the living room, and we prayed, "Jesus, will you change the hearts of his parents so he can go to church with us and learn of you?" After that prayer, he came back from asking his parents and went to church with us. They saw God in action. He answered our prayers. He says, *"Ask anything and I will answer, as long as it is within His will"* (Matthew 7:7). My children are all serving the Lord. Someday, they will lead in a way that will make me so proud. Not that I am not proud now; I just know they will take the mantle and double it.

Maybe we should reach out to families who are hurting and pray for them. Take them into your intercessory prayer time and ask Christ to lead them to the light. We should all help set up programs that will help them focus on what is important to Christ, like counseling, the Four Commands of Christ, and governing values. Something that they can lean on and use to establish their relationship with Christ. It is my experience that, if we follow the Four Commands of Christ faithfully, then our whole universe around us will change.

Wouldn't it be grand if we, Christians, went into the community where we live and started praying for our neighbors? Ask them what their needs are and if we could pray for them for that need. An army of Christians praying for the community. Wow, I am excited just writing about it.

Our purpose on earth is to glorify God. We glorify Him in our love for each other. Forgive others, especially your brother and sister in Christ that attend your church and community. People who want Christ in their lives but are hesitant to come because of the Church's reputation needs to be changed by us. We need to love one another. Practice forgiveness.

Chapter Four

Fourth Command: Live Your Mission

*"Then Jesus came to them and said, 'All authority in heaven
and on earth has been given to me. Therefore, go and make
disciples of all nations, baptizing them in the name of the
Father and of the Son and of the Holy Spirit, and teaching
them to obey everything I have commanded you. And surely,
I am with you always, to the very end of the age.'"*

Matthew 28:18-20

The Fourth Command of Christ is otherwise known as "the Great
Commission." Why do I call it a command of Christ? Because of
the words, "Therefore, go!" We cannot consider ourselves disciples of
Christ if we are not willing to lovingly spread His gospel to the world
and disciple all peoples and nations. We need to disciple people into a
relationship with Jesus Christ using the Four Commands of Christ as
the basis of education and following the spiritual disciplines. Each and
every one of us is responsible for spreading the Good News. Not just
our pastors, not just our missionaries, but all of us. You have read this
book thus far, and I am grateful for this, but now we need to wake up
to our mission in life here on earth.

Jesus died on the cross so God could accept us into heaven by the blood of Jesus that covers us. Not by works but by Faith. He did not make this a hard thing; come as you are and let Christ work miracles in your life. Christ's death and resurrection are full of nothing but holiness, power, and love for His creation. If you abide (believe in) in Him, then God only sees the blood that His Son shed for us, covering our sins and making us acceptable to Him, thus sanctifying (grafting) us into His family.[45] Nothing else should reside in us but His holiness (Be holy for I am holy). The operative word here is *if* we follow Him! We can only become citizens of heaven and be in the presence of God if we are holy. We can only be holy if Jesus is in our hearts, minds, and soul, and we give him our money, energy, effort, and time. After all, what is our mission in life as Christians while we are on this earth? It is not the purpose-driven life; it is the mission-driven life. Let me share some of the Scriptures that have shaped my thoughts on this:

> *Speak to the entire congregation of the Israelites and tell them: Be holy because I, the LORD your God, am holy. (Leviticus 19:2)*

> *And there will be a highway called the Way of Holiness. The unclean will not travel it, only those who walk in that Way— and fools will not stray onto it. (Isaiah 35:8)*

> *Enter through the narrow gate; for the gate is wide and the way is broad that leads to destruction, and there are many who enter through it. For the gate is small and the way is narrow that leads to life, and there are few who find it. (Matthew 7:13-14 NASB)*

---

45 John 15:7

If some of the branches have been broken off, and you,
though a wild olive shoot, have been grafted in among the
others and now share in the nourishing sap from the olive
root. (Romans 11:17)

In the final verse, the main olive tree is Israel, and when they as a nation sin, branches are broken off. Gentiles are considered the wild olive shoot and are grafted in by being born again.

We are grafted into fellowship with God through Christ; therefore, we are ambassadors for Christ, are we not? But if we deny Christ and live as everyone else does, this is what Jesus says will happen:

The ax lies ready at the root of the [olive] trees, and every
[olive and wild olive] tree that does not produce good fruit
will be cut down and thrown into the fire. (Matthew 3:10)

Yes, some of you are living as you should. But some of you are living just by the seat of your pants with one foot in Heaven and one foot in this world, and some of you are not following Christ at all. I call this person CHRINO. You go to church and may even serve on the church board, but you do not practice holiness or God's commands. Some people have moved so far away from our Creator that they have become lost. So lost, in fact, that some will not make it back. I am so thankful that God decided that I would be saved in 1969. This relationship with a holiness church has shaped my thinking throughout my life. Thank you, Lord, for life. Have I lived the holy life? Sometimes yes and sometimes no. And sometimes I've lived it by the seat of my pants, too. I wrote this book in in hopes of keeping some of you from making the same mistakes that I have made.

The times we are in today require us to move closer to God in holiness. We need to move closer to Christ right now, sooner rather than later.[46] Some will say that living a holy life is impossible. We are

---

46 John 9:4

sinners, and that is why Jesus has covered us with His blood. Satan will always remind us of our sins and of how worthless we are until we are worn out and give in. Satan is always telling us that it's dumb to try to live a holy life.

Deep inside, some of us may be worried that we will be made fun of, teased, and, yes, even considered stupid for trying to be the Christian man or woman we want to be. Some will tell lies about us, trying to destroy our witness to others. At one point in my life, I was surrounded by people who were just like that. When I was at the beginning of my walk with Jesus, there were people who I once considered friends who sent a very beautiful young lady to my apartment with the intention of seducing me to sin. I told her to leave, but before she left, I presented the gospel to her. I asked her if she wanted to accept Jesus into her life. Of course, she left right away, and I thanked God that I was worthy to be tested. I have stayed away from those so-called friends to this day. I hope and pray that one of them has accepted Christ because of that testimony.

There will always be people who will say we cannot walk in holiness unto the Lord; after all, we are human, and only Christ was able to walk in holiness. While this is true, when we accept Jesus into our hearts, He deposits the Holy Spirit in us and sanctifies us immediately. At that exact moment we have the power to overcome sin. The problem is sin nature, Satan, and sometimes the Christian community, who are the ones who steal your joy and power. Only through the covering of His blood and the power of the Holy Spirit are we able to walk in faith, love, and success. If we walk defeated, we will live defeated. Stand up against Satan and his lies about you. Walk in the Power of the Holy Spirit. We are cleansed of any and all sin when we accept Christ. God doesn't even know what we are talking about when we revisit our sin in our mind. Our sin was already paid for at the cross so don't allow others to steal your joy. We are redeemed and sealed by what Christ did at the cross. Develop a spiritual formation to overcome the world and the lies that Satan feeds you. You need to look at holiness and Christian perfection as your main goal in life. This can only be realized if you are in the zone with Christ.

We should set standards for ourselves to achieve the goal of holiness, even if it seems out of reach. As part of my construction career, I have received extensive training from the Occupational Safety and Health Administration (OSHA). Their goal is to have no more deaths in the industry. Is that attainable? Maybe not, but they set standards to try and attain that goal anyway. They exact very large fines for not adopting the standards they have set to achieve that goal. Why shouldn't we be just as aggressive? Remember, greater is He who is in you than he who is in the world. If you determine that your governing value will be Christian perfection, then you can accomplish this or at least be on the straight and narrow road trying to accomplish this by using the Four Commands of Christ and following the spiritual disciplines. You, with the help of the Holy Spirit, can be an overcomer and be in the zone.

We need to transcend above all Christian denominations and understand the Four Commands of Christ as an *interdenominational* way to worship Christ. The Four Commands of Christ say it all. Rather, I should say that Jesus says it all: ALL the prophets and ALL the Law are summed up in these first two commands.[47] I have simply packaged these four commands to express Jesus's direction for us all as He directed me. Let's not quibble over who has the way and who does not, denominationally speaking. Jesus said, "*I am the way, the truth, and the life.*" Only through Christ do we find salvation and only in His name. There is only one requirement: "*Believe and be holy for I am holy*" (1 Peter 1:15-16).

So, how do we work on being holy?

But someone will say, "You have faith; I have deeds." Show me your faith without deeds, and I will show you my faith by my deeds. You believe that there is one God. Good! Even the demons believe that—and shudder. You foolish person, do you want evidence that faith without deeds is useless? Was not our father Abraham considered righteous for what he did when he offered his son Isaac on the altar? You see that his faith and his actions were working together, and his faith was made complete by what he did. And the scripture

---

47 Matthew 7:12

was fulfilled that says, "Abraham believed God, and it was credited to him as righteousness," and he was called God's friend. You see that a person is considered righteous by what they do and not by faith alone. (James 2:18-24)

James is saying, "Show me your faith, and I will show you my deeds (works), or show me your deeds (works), and I will show you my faith." They must go hand in hand. Believing in Jesus is your faith and following His commands is the deeds (works).[48] The spiritual disciplines you adopt into your life will help you maintain your relationship with Jesus and put you in the zone: humbling yourself, submitting, giving your neighbor grace, mercy, and forgiveness, and spreading the gospel. Reading your Bible will show you how to behave and prepare for the end times.

While Jesus was sitting on the Mount of Olives, the disciples came to Him privately. "Tell us," they said, "when will these things happen, and what will be the sign of Your coming and of the end of the age?" Jesus answered, "See to it that no one deceives you. For many will come in My name, claiming, 'I am the Christ,' and will deceive many. You will hear of wars and rumors of wars but see to it that you are not alarmed. These things must happen, but the end is still to come. Nation will rise against nation, and kingdom against kingdom. There will be famines and earthquakes in various places. All these are the beginning of birth pains. Then they will deliver you over to be persecuted and killed, and you will be hated by all nations because of My name. At that time many will fall away and will betray and hate one another, and many false prophets will arise and mislead many. Because of the multiplication of wickedness, the love

---

48 John 14:15

of most will grow cold. But the one who perseveres to the end will be saved. And this gospel of the kingdom will be preached in all the world as a testimony to all nations, and then the end will come." (Matthew 24:3-14 NASB)

I see the birth pains all over the place, even more so now than when I started writing this book five years ago. There are earthquakes, tsunamis, wildfires, tornadoes, and active volcanoes everywhere across this world. There are wars and rumors of wars everywhere. Society is trying to push all of us into a one-world government, starting with global accords that tie up the unique freedoms that Americans have. Even among our own citizens, there are agents trying to make America the bane of the world. They think we should bow down and apologize to others since we were the aggressors, the contaminators of the world. They twist our words of freedom and try to make us look guilty and wrong in the world's courts of thought and deeds. What is right and virtuous has now been twisted into being wrong and hateful. The world is trying to become a one-world government without God. Through lies, deceit, and propaganda, the governments are now saying that they know better than you and that you either share their way of thinking or are a criminal. They are trying to tell you how you should act, what you should eat, what you should drink, and how you are to live your life. They want to dictate what you believe and in whom you believe. They do not want the real church to have any say in this. They are using global warming, gun control, and health insurance as a way to divide Americans and take control of our nation. Other countries do not have the same freedoms we have because they do not have our constitution. So, those countries are pushing us, the United States, into a single socialistic society; capitalism is out, and socialism is in. If we give in, then all of us—Christians and non-Christians alike—will lose our rights and capacity to pursue happiness. Take my word for it: the end is coming and not too far in the future. Maybe sooner than we have all thought. I am here to tell you that we are in the birth pains of the End Times. *"As long as it is day, we must do the works of him who sent me. Night is coming, when no one can work"* (John 9:4). Go and share Christ while there is light.

I have been commissioned by Jesus to tell everyone that this is the time to get ready for His second coming: *"Son of man, I have made you a watchman for the people of Israel; so hear the word I speak and give them warning from me"* (Ezekiel 3:17). Accept Jesus in your heart today. This is the day, not tomorrow. None of us know when our time will be up. When it does come, if you are not in Christ, then you are lost forever. There is no other way to change the outcome.

We need to warn everyone we come in contact with that Christ will be coming someday and someday soon. Non-Christians need to have Jesus in their heart before it is too late, and Christians who have become cold need revival. God says He has set before us life (heaven) and death (hell). Choose life.

> *"This day I call the heavens and the earth as witnesses against you that I have set before you life and death, blessings and curses. Now choose life, so that you and your children may live* [20] *and that you may love the Lord your God, listen to his voice, and hold fast to him. For the Lord is your life, and he will give you many years in the land he swore to give to your fathers, Abraham, Isaac and Jacob."*
> *(Deuteronomy 30:19-20)*

Jesus is telling us in advance that night is coming, meaning when that day comes and the rapture has happened, those who are left will no longer have the ability to reach out to Jesus. We are taught in this Scripture that, once we die, we either go to heaven or hell. Jesus does not send us there; we send ourselves there by how we live. This is important to understand. He asks all of us Christians to tell everyone who do not believe and who will listen about heaven and hell.

There was a rich man who was dressed in purple and fine linen and lived in luxury every day. At his gate was laid a beggar named Lazarus, covered with sores and longing to eat what fell from the rich man's table. Even the dogs came and licked his sores. The time came when the beggar died and the angels carried him to Abraham's side. The rich man also died and was buried. In Hades, where he was in torment, he looked up and saw Abraham far away, with Lazarus by his side. So, he called to him, "Father Abraham, have pity on me and send Lazarus to dip the tip of his finger in water and cool my tongue, because I am in agony in this fire." But Abraham replied, "Son, remember that in your lifetime you received your good things, while Lazarus received bad things, but now he is comforted here and you are in agony. And besides all this, between us and you a great chasm has been set in place, so that those who want to go from here to you cannot, nor can anyone cross over from there to us." He answered, "Then I beg you, Father, send Lazarus to my family, for I have five brothers. Let him warn them, so that they will not also come to this place of torment." Abraham replied, "They have Moses and the Prophets; let them listen to them." "No, Father Abraham," he said, "but if someone from the dead goes to them, they will repent." He said to him, "If they do not listen to Moses and the Prophets, they will not be convinced even if someone rises from the dead." (Luke 16:19-31)

The story of Lazarus is full of truth and knowledge. After all, Jesus did rise from the dead, and people still do not believe in Him or worship Him. If this story doesn't move you to want eternity in heaven, then what will? I am here to tell you that life matters, and Christ wants the best for us. Someone needs to tell you the truth about the universe, about life on earth, and about your soul, which is eternal. Someone needs to teach you how you to overcome life's pressures and the roller coaster of existence. The most important point is how much God loves you and wants to help you navigate through life until He comes for you.

We have become so divided that an extraordinarily small proportion of people on this earth know the way to truth. It seems to me that very few are subjugating their thoughts and rights to God and instead have enslaved themselves to the new politically correct dogma. There is only one absolute truth: Jesus Christ died on the cross and was raised from the dead to bring us new life, the only life that will get us into heaven. No one can take this truth away from those of us who truly believe in Christ.

Now, my first appeal is to all those who have a heart for Jesus, but are not practicing what they know to be true: turn from that mindset. If you are drawn by the Holy Spirit through reading this, I would suggest strongly that you get on your knees and adopt the Four Commands of Christ. You may not be living for Christ at this moment, and that's okay, but please start looking to Christ for your salvation. Come as you are.[49]

My second appeal is to those whose hearts God will change if we pray the intercessor's prayer for them. Our holy mission while we are alive on this earth is to share Jesus, live a holy life, and spread the Good News to the world. This is why we all need to share the Fourth Command of Christ; we do not know who will be called and accept Jesus. Let us all learn how to live a life pleasing to Jesus in being discipled. Then raise our children to do the same and then go out into our neighborhood and spread the Good News, our mission in life.

> *Then the master told his servant, "Go out to the roads and country lanes and compel them to come in, so that my house will be full. I tell you, not one of those who were invited will get a taste of my banquet." (Luke 14:23)*

---

49 Joel 2:32

We are therefore Christ's ambassadors, as though God were making his appeal through us. We implore you on Christ's behalf: Be reconciled to God. (2 Corinthians 5:20)

These passages compel us to (1) be in Christ, (2) be ambassadors for Christ, and (3) share Christ with the world, especially to our neighbor. Jesus also gave us another parable, written by the Apostle Matthew to teach us our mission in life.

Jesus spoke to them again in parables, saying: "The kingdom of heaven is like a king who prepared a wedding banquet for his son. He sent his servants to those who had been invited to the banquet to tell them to come, but they refused to come. Then he sent some more servants and said, 'Tell those who have been invited that I have prepared my dinner: My oxen and fattened cattle have been butchered, and everything is ready. Come to the wedding banquet.' But they paid no attention and went off—one to his field, another to his business. The rest seized his servants, mistreated them and killed them. The king was enraged. He sent his army and destroyed those murderers and burned their city. Then he said to his servants, 'The wedding banquet is ready, but those I invited did not deserve to come. So go to the street corners and invite to the banquet anyone you find.' So, the servants went out into the streets and gathered all the people they could find, the bad as well as the good, and the wedding hall was filled with guests. But when the king came in to see the guests, he noticed a man there who was not wearing wedding clothes. He asked, 'How did you get in here without wedding clothes, friend?' The man was speechless. Then the king told the attendants, 'Tie him hand and foot, and throw him outside, into the darkness, where there will be weeping and gnashing of teeth. 'For many are invited, but few are chosen." (Matthew 22:1-4)

This parable of the banquet tells us what we as Christians should be working towards: inviting people to the wedding banquet that is coming. It also tells us who will enter heaven and who will not. Inviting people to accept Jesus as their savior is our mission in life as Christians. All of us should equip ourselves for this mission as we go along in daily life.

We don't seem to be able to share Christ because there is always something in our lives that condemns us, and we fear being seen as hypocrites. We have allowed a wall to remain between us and God. We have not learned to break down that wall, and we keep selling ourselves short and remain quiet about Christ. Because of Satan's continual attack on us, we believe that it is not our job or we are not equipped to share the gospel. Jesus has equipped us to share the gospel through the Holy Spirit just by using or telling our story. We need to be bold and move forward.

Have I not commanded you? Be strong and courageous. Do not be afraid; do not be discouraged, for the LORD your God will be with you wherever you go. (Joshua 1:9)

Pray and ask Jesus what method He would like to see you use to share Christ with your neighbor. One method is to use your life story and the Four Commands of Christ to reach our neighbors.

We need to make Christianity something that is not difficult to grasp but attainable. In Deuteronomy 30:11, God tells the new Nation of Israel, *"Now what I am commanding you today is not too difficult for you or beyond your reach."* God was telling Israel to learn His commandments and graft them into their lives. God reaffirmed this to Israel after 760 years through Isaiah. In Isaiah 45:19, He tells Isaiah to write this: *"I have not spoken in secret, in a dark place of the earth: I said not unto the seed of Jacob, Seek ye me in vain: I the LORD speak righteousness, I declare things that are right."*

Jesus is telling us today that it is not too hard for us to grasp. The

Four Commands of Christ are short, direct, and concise. The instructions on how to apply them to our lives are also short, direct, and concise.

I remember as a new Christian having more questions than answers. God eventually answered all my questions, but it took time, mainly because of my lack of maturity, lack of concentration, and my lack of time spent with Him. I think they call this lack of discipline. It has taken me a lifetime to acquire and use what I have learned in Christianity toward His Glory and hopefully your gain. Some people just are not aware of the consequences of their decisions they make for their lives. It is up to us as Christians to lovingly explain to them the options that are available to them: life or death for eternity. Once people have decided to follow Jesus, they need training. The expressions of faith will help each of you to perfect your spiritual formation. We need to figure out what our governing values are so we can attain the goals that God instilled in us when we were knitted together in our mother's womb.[50]

Perseverance is what Paul said we should practice; let's go and share Christ with others so they can win the spiritual race with us, too. If we practice and teach what is important to Christ, then we will be in the zone, and our neighbor will be in the zone, and we will all win the race. It is the *pursuit of Christian perfection* that counts. It is an attitude of the heart, not outward works but inward works. Circumcision of the heart.[51] Love of the Lord with all—and I mean *all*—of our heart, soul, mind, and strength. If we communicate the Four Commands of Christ, then we won't be confused in life and will be willing to share Christ.

We need to set the bar as high as the heavens, to set goals that are lofty and then persevere until the day Christ returns. Setting a goal to work toward Holiness is attainable. Otherwise, Christ would not say *be holy because I am holy* or *be perfect as your father in heaven is perfect.* Some may say to themselves, "Why bother? I am a sinner and cannot change." This is Satan talking to you, not Christ. Do not listen. We can work toward holiness by applying the Four Commands of Christ in our daily life. Go out and live your mission.

---

50 Psalm 139:13
51 Romans 2:29

PART TWO

Spiritual Disciplines

Chapter 5

Know You Are Eternal

"By the sweat of your brow you will eat your food until you return to the ground, since from it you were taken; for dust you are and to dust you will return."

Genesis 3:19

I have always thought that if people knew the truth about their eternity, then maybe they would be more apt to believe in God, the creator of everything. And I think a major reason why so many people do not believe in God is because some in the Christian community have lost their first love: education. We have lost control of the educational system, which won't allow creation to be taught anywhere. If you were to bring up creation in class, you would be ostracized and put in the dunce corner.

There are people who believe in a god, and some believe in multiple gods. Some believe in reincarnation, and some have a spiritual awareness of themselves but not of a Creator God. Then there are atheists, who have their own form of religion: religion of self. They say they do not believe in a god, but doesn't that require faith? They say they have no dogma, yet they file lawsuits against schools for teaching religion. Why should they care? If it is because they don't want their children taught religion, then maybe they should start their own schools. Their approach is religious in its nature. Atheists and Christians both have belief systems; they have just directed it differently. Both require faith. You can't prove there is a God, but I believe I can.

God said in Genesis, "Let us make man in our own image." There is God the Father, God the Son, and God the Holy Spirit. Man and woman have a body, soul, and spirit. We are the only living creature in the universe that have a soul and spirit. God determined what good and evil is in His Bible. Everyone knows that there is good and evil but only because God defined it, not us. Our moral fortitude is instilled in us when we are born. Love is His nature, and He alone defines life and the abundance of life. He alone is asking His creation to listen to the rules that have been in place since before time.

The ones who do believe in God also have different views on what they believe. Some churches say you must believe this way or that way, and some individuals believe God is holy, but we will never be able to achieve a holy life. If you were to take all the beliefs, stories, fables, myths, and folklore throughout time, you will see a common thread: our Creator God who is everlasting, spiritual, and all powerful.

We see this in Hebrew names for God, including *Elohim, Jehovah, El-Shaddai,* and *Adonai,* which reflect might and strength. Greek fables depict how Satan and his minions have committed ugly actions here on earth, where misfit angels mate with humanity and create mythological beings. The North American Indians believe in what they call "the Great Spirit" and believe that, when they die, they go to that great hunting ground. Some cannibals believed if they would eat humans, the spirit they ate would be absorbed into their bodies and become a part of them. In some societies, humans were sacrificed on altars to please the spirits they worshiped.

Throughout history, people have believed in a higher power. My God is the creator of the heavens and the earth. In six days, He created all that we can see, touch, taste, hear, and smell and even more that is beyond our senses or knowledge. In Genesis, Moses tells us that God formed man out of the dust of the earth and blew His breath (spirit) into man to make him a living being. This is where our soul and spirit comes from, which makes us totally different than any other creature in all of creation.

Most of the world believes in a god that is eternal, just not YHWH. Now, if God spoke into existence the universe and all things in it and then He blew His breath into man, then all of creation, including man, is eternal. Why? Because God is eternal.

> *Remember Him before the silver cord is snapped and the*
> *golden bowl is crushed, before the pitcher is shattered at*
> *the spring and the wheel is broken at the well, before the*
> *dust returns to the ground from which it came and the spirit*
> *returns to God who gave it. (Ecclesiastes12:6-7)*

God created all that is in existence in six days and then rested on the seventh day. When God breathed life into man, we became eternal beings: our soul will never die. Now we need to worry about where this eternal soul will live. The soul lives in a body for a short time and then returns to either heaven or hell. God has given us free will, and basically, we decide our destiny.

Throughout the Bible, God defines life and death for us. To believe in Jesus is life; to not believe is death. There is a physical death, and there is a spiritual death. The second death, for lack of a better term, is eternally devastating, and the agony of it will never end.

> *Whoever has ears, let them hear what the Spirit says to the*
> *churches. The one who is victorious will not be hurt at all by*
> *the second death. (Revelation 2:11)*

> *The sea gave up its dead, and Death and Hades gave up*
> *their dead, and each one was judged according to his deeds.*
> *Then Death and Hades were thrown into the lake of fire.*
> *This is the second death—the lake of fire. And if anyone was*

*found whose name was not written in the Book of Life, he
was thrown into the lake of fire. (Revelation 20:13-15)*

God made the lake of fire (hell) for Satan and the fallen angels, not
for man. Since Adam and Eve sinned in the garden, humans are no
longer guaranteed eternal life with God. When anyone goes before the
throne of God and their name is not written in the Book of Life, they
are sent to the eternal lake of fire.

You are eternal, and you need to know that there are only two places
created by God for His creation to go: heaven or hell. I know some do
not want to hear this, but someone has to stand up and tell you the truth.
Hell is a reality. Since Satan was cast out of heaven and thrown down
to this universe, we all live in a corrupted world. Satan was thrown out
of heaven because of pride. He would not humble himself and submit,
he would not give grace and mercy to his neighbor as himself, and he
would not forgive or repent. There was a time when Lucifer walked
closely with God. Then pride took over, and he sinned.

*You were blameless in your ways from the day you were cre-
ated till wickedness was found in you. (Ezekiel 28:11-19)*

*The fool says in his heart, "There is no God." They are cor-
rupt, and their ways are vile; there is no one who does good.
God looks down from heaven on all mankind to see if there
are any who understand, any who seek God. Everyone has
turned away, all have become corrupt; there is no one who
does good, not even one. (Psalm 53:1-3)*

We are eternal beings, so we need to address our state of mind and
soul. We need to examine ourselves and decide who we are as individuals.
Life is difficult enough as it is and is made much more difficult without
Christ. God is always working for us, protecting us, helping us, and
answering our prayers and questions. I am making a plea for your soul
right now. As many have said before me, "If I, as a born-again Christian,

am wrong about eternity, then I have lost nothing, but if I am right, you have lost everything."

People have a hard time believing in and worshipping a God they cannot see. I am so sorry for these who will not listen because they do not know what they are doing. Should you accept the teaching of these Four Commands of Christ, you will change inside. It will get you ready for heaven and teach you how to share Christ's gospel. I can tell you from experience that He is alive and well and deserves our praise. He deserves our loyalty. He deserves to be Glorified. He deserves every part of who we are and more. He deserves your attention. Know that you are eternal and you decide your eternal home. I implore you to choose life.

Chapter 6

Commit to Jesus

"Without holiness no one will see the Lord."

Hebrews 12:14

Throughout history, God has taught His creation what is important to Him and how to maintain a relationship with Him. He has also laid down what not to do, the actions that would separate us from Him. As author John Piper said, *"Every human being in the world has an inborn knowledge of God and his law."*[52] How long will we continue in ignorance of the Mighty God that made everything we see, hear, taste, touch, and smell?

Humanity is born with an innate desire to do good but also wants to cheat to get ahead in life. Socrates, who was working on the meaning and value of virtue, asked his followers to examine their lives and test whether their life was moral. If it had value, should humanity adopt it, and not just some of it but all of it? My opinion is he was looking for Christ, but unfortunately, the Messiah had not come into the world yet, and his fellow Greeks were steeped in false gods.

We are born with the law of God on our hearts, but sin nature is also working to destroy it. When we grow up without direction and guidance, we lose sight of what is moral. We seem to let the influence

---

52 https://www.desiringgod.org/interviews/how-is-the-law-written-on-every-heart

of the devil and immoral friends guide our footsteps. This is why we need to be careful who our children hang out with and who we hang out with. We need to make sure everything we put before us and surround ourselves with is holy. Paul talked about this in Romans:

> *Indeed, when gentiles, who do not have the law, do by nature what the law requires, they are a law to themselves, even though they do not have the law, Since they show that the work of the Law is written on their hearts, their consciences also bearing witness, and their thoughts either accusing or defending them. (Romans 2:14-15)*

These gems are interspersed throughout the Bible. Most of us believe in God or a god; we are just not sure of the true God. We don't know who has the correct approach. Some say go this way; some say go that way. This is why we need to teach everyone we come in contact with who and why Jesus Christ was crucified for us. In discipling as we go through life, we will explore this together and try to solve this mystery.

Man's carnal nature comes from the fall in the garden. It is obvious that, since man became rebellious, those who follow after him from generation to generation are rebellious, too. This is sin nature, and we are all born with it. For most people, it is easier and more fun to give into their carnal nature (sin nature), especially when they are young. Going with the crowd fills that void in your life, and it becomes normal. Then, when tragedy hits, you look to God for help, but you are not sure if He cares enough for you. So, you quit and live in that mire of pain and agony. If you would only turn your heart toward Christ, He would answer in a millisecond with the Holy Spirit, filling your heart with His love. Your problems may not be solved, but the agony is. Christ fills your soul with peace. This is the best time to be discipled. When Christ is in your heart, use the Four Commands of Christ and the spiritual disciplines to begin your journey with Christ.

There are many examples of people who have succumbed to sin and ended up with addictions of some sort: sex, drugs, pornography, drinking, computer games, work, partying, social media, making money. They might say in their mind that their future and time is more important than a life and relationship with Jesus, that they don't want to give it up yet. Some people may get so wrapped up in their sin that they do not want to accept any kind of change. Plenty of famous people, who would seem to have it all, have died from alcoholism or suicide and had multiple marriages because they couldn't satisfy their soul. They couldn't or wouldn't find help in Christ. People don't make a commitment to better themselves because they don't want to give up what they have; they fail to realize what they have lasts only a season. Sin is fun for a time; then it sneaks up on you, and you become its slave.

People do not realize until it is too late that they are addicted to the habit they have developed. My wife and I have known many people who have given in to their desires and ended up losing everything. They left their home, spouse, and children to pursue some addicted person who seemed to be more attractive. They quickly become addicted with them and end up living on the street or getting in trouble with the law. Some people cannot change even if they want to because they have given over to their desires and have become so addicted they cannot form a moral path anymore.

When I was sixteen and living in Springville, California, I was at the Nazarene Church when Jesus gloriously saved me. He actually was present and touched me on my head. He was brilliantly white, blazing in all His glory. I screamed inside with a joy that I have never felt since that day. I wished I would have screamed out loud for everyone to hear, but I quickly thought about how embarrassed I might be. I eventually cooled off from that encounter. When I read in Revelations that if I was hot or cold, He could deal with me, but if I was lukewarm, he would spit me out of His mouth, I was overcome with such fear that I quit being a Christian. I walked away from all that Jesus gave me through salvation. Even though I was gloriously saved, I still quit. No one in my church knew how to disciple me. Oh, they would counsel me and say change your ways, but how?

I became a sinner like everyone else I hung out with at the time. I put all my responsibilities aside. I turned to the world to support my cravings. I had a goal that I would become a contractor and a real estate agent by the time I was twenty-five. I met that goal and became a very successful contractor/developer. I developed lots and sold houses that everyone could afford at the time. I did very well until 1980 hit, and interest rates climbed to 22 percent. I eventually was able to sell all the houses and all the lots and even the land that I had acquired, but after paying back all the investors I had sought out to help keep me afloat, there was nothing left for me. I was broke. I mean broke. I had nothing left. I lost it all, and my self-esteem went with it.

I finally gave in and turned to Jesus to save me. He came to me again without abandon. He filled my heart with joy, and I entered a new beginning for myself. Interestingly, one of the very large subdivisions I had built wrapped around the church denomination I was saved in at sixteen years old when Christ touched me. I turned to that church for help. They did not know how to handle a man like me, but they really put the welcome mat out. These were older folks who were full of the Holy Spirit and who loved Jesus and life more than I can explain in words. They took me under their wings and just loved me. When I was hungry, they fed me. When I was lonely, they let me join them in Bible study and prayer meetings. They made me such a part of their family that I worked hard for them in building a huge church that was free and clear of any debt. The church was built by the members.

Some people just will not do what it takes to change. Their hearts become like stones, seared by the hot iron of apathy. They like where they are and don't believe God will help them to change the circumstances they are surrounded by or they are too proud to turn to Him. They blame God for all their troubles. They say to themselves, "Why would God allow this incident to happen to me? If He was a loving God, I wouldn't be here. What kind of God allows this stuff to go on and hurt so many?" Some just flat-out do not believe, so they develop their own reasons to hate God. Some may have accepted Jesus at some time in their life, most likely when they were young, but as they grew older, they allowed themselves to cool off. Either they don't know how to stay in the zone or they were not taught (discipled). They give up because life is too hard for them. They have not seen the miracles that God does or say it is for everyone else but not for them. No one has shown them the straight and narrow way, or they don't have the discipline to walk it.

Jesus told a story about this called the Parable of the Sower.

That same day Jesus went out of the house and sat by the lake. Such large crowds gathered around him that he got into a boat and sat in it, while all the people stood on the shore. Then he told them many things in parables, saying: "A farmer went out to sow his seed. As he was scattering the seed, some fell along the path, and the birds came and ate it up. Some fell on rocky places, where it did not have much soil. It sprang up quickly, because the soil was shallow. But when the sun came up, the plants were scorched, and they withered because they had no root. Other seed fell among thorns, which grew up and choked the plants. Still other seed fell on good soil, where it produced a crop—a hundred, sixty or thirty times what was sown. Whoever has ears, let them hear... Listen then to what the parable of the Sower means: When anyone hears the message about the kingdom and does not understand it, the evil one comes and snatches away what was sown in their heart. This is the seed sown along the path. The seed falling on rocky ground refers to someone who hears the word and at once receives it with joy. But since they have no root, they last only a short time. When trouble or persecution comes because of the word, they quickly fall away. The seed falling among the thorns refers to someone who hears the word, but the worries of this life and the deceitfulness of wealth choke the word, making it unfruitful. But the seed falling on good soil refers to someone who hears the word and understands it. This is the one who produces a crop, yielding a hundred, sixty or thirty times what was sown. (Mark 4:10)

We know that our human nature does not react to the word of God like we would hope or think it should. Our human nature wants to shy away from any associations with the Holy Spirit. Why are we not able to see the forest for the trees? Why are we sometimes unwilling to examine our lives and find truth?

I think Plato's allegorical story of the cave may help us understand this aversion to truth. People are chained to their own perception of what life is and won't look at any other concept or reality. If they grew up a certain way, then that is how they will live. No truth seems to matter. If only their chains were broken and they were able to leave the cave and see the sun (and the Son), what a wonderful world this would be. *"Start children off on the way they should go, and even when they are old they will not turn from it"* (Proverbs 22:6).

When will we examine ourselves and find out if we measure up to God's requirements? Should we weigh the scales? Will we find that we are short of the goal? When do we start looking for the truth? The problem is that we have so many ways to measure that we become confused about which path to take. Each of us is chained down to our upbringing. We are convinced that this is the way when in reality it is not. If we don't find Christianity the way Jesus teaches it, we may become delusional about Christianity and give up.

Many people and even some churches adopt the "my way or the highway" mentality. If you don't do this or do that, then you are not a Christian. We need to unchain ourselves to any dogma and let the Holy Spirit teach us His way. Doesn't Jesus say be holy because I am holy? How can we be Holy?

> *Therefore, with minds that are alert and fully sober, set your*
> *hope on the grace to be brought to you when Jesus Christ is*
> *revealed at his coming. As obedient children do not conform*
> *to the evil desires you had when you lived in ignorance. But*
> *just as He who called you is holy, so be holy in all you do; for*
> *it is written: "Be holy, because I am holy." (1 Peter 1:13-16)*

*Speak to all the congregation of the sons of Israel and say
to them, "You shall be holy, for I the LORD your God am
holy." (Leviticus 19:2)*

Worshipping God in a way that is ancient but relevant is what this
book is all about but also direct and to the point. What matters is what
Jesus said to His disciples before and after going to heaven. *Wait for
the Holy Spirit and go and disciple all nations.* All of His commands
are summed up in the Four Commands of Christ. I packaged it as I was
told, and it requires our attention. Yes, these are strong words, but all
of us—including myself—need to listen.

It is my hope and wish that all who read this will examine themselves
and not get stuck in their own dogma or church dogma. Let's allow the
Holy Spirit to move us toward Christ and what Christ thinks is important.
I am not saying we should change our churches. I am saying, however,
that we need to begin walking with Jesus toward holiness. Can we all
agree that the ultimate goal in life is to be with Jesus in heaven? If this
is our goal, then we must strive for Christian perfection. Jesus says for
that to happen, we must be humble and submit. We must show mercy
and grace. We must forgive everyone. Those of us who have faith in
Christ are holy because of the blood of Christ. He makes us acceptable
to God. He is our high priest. So, we must also continue in our quest
to be like Jesus. We must take up our cross and follow Him. We must
die daily to ourselves and walk toward Him.

In 1 Samuel 13:14 it is written, *"The LORD has sought a man after
His own heart."* God said this to Samuel about a man named David,
who would be the future king of Israel. But as king, David was an
adulterer and a murderer, and because he counted the fighting men of
Israel, he caused 25,000 Israelites to die. He did not always do what
God told him to do, and sometimes he did exactly what God told him
to do. Why would God say that David was a man after His own heart?
Because David was always asking God for forgiveness. He would wrap
his arms around the horns of the altar and beg for forgiveness. David
would always strive and work toward being holy. Psalm 51 describes
one of the most beautiful ways of asking for forgiveness. It also explains

what God does to the one who asks for forgiveness. It is known that the straight and narrow road leads to righteousness, so let this be the path you take. Don't gamble with your life.

I would like anyone who is reading this right now and who does not have an ongoing relationship with Christ to ask Him into your heart right now. Ask Jesus to forgive you of your sins, whatever they may be. Use Psalm 51 as your prayer and then thank Him profusely for filling you with His Holy Spirit. For any of you who have fallen, pick yourself up by saying the same prayer. Those whose light has gone out, say the same prayer, and Jesus will relight the way for you, oh so bright. Remember what I said about straight and narrow and being disciplined? Work the Four Commands as you would in any sports training regimen. Follow the expressions of faith as your training, and when you have trained for a while, watch Jesus bless your life.

Thank you, Jesus, for calling us back to you. Now help all of us to overcome. Amen.

Chapter 7

Get on Your Knees and Pray

"Very early in the morning, while it was still dark, Jesus got up, left the house and went off to a solitary place, where he prayed."

Mark 1:35

How do you begin your day? How you begin your day is an especially important part of Christian discipline, according to the Bible. Why not mimic and adopt what Daniel did every day? Read about how God saved him from the lion's den, how he promoted him in the eyes of the people in power who ruled over him and Israel.

It is important that we follow our Savior, our mentor, our king, Jesus. Jesus started His days early in the morning and always in prayer. He would go somewhere out of the way and pray alone. In the Book of Matthew, Jesus takes Peter, John, and James alone to pray, and boy, did they pray. Jesus transfigured into His glorious body, Elijah and Moses appeared, and God spoke from heaven to the apostles: *"This is my Son whom I love, and with Him I am well pleased. Listen to him!"* (Matthew 17:5).

I think we sometimes can't see the forest for the trees when it comes to prayer because we have allowed our lives to be so busy. The transfiguration is one of the pivotal points of Christianity. It is held in such high esteem, as it should be, but did it overshadow God's last words to us? Have we all missed the entire communication? At the end of His proclamation of His love for His Son, He said, "Listen to Him." Listening also includes actions, like praying, memorizing Scripture, reading the Bible, fasting, and spending time with Him. I would say that prayer should be our standard hallmark of Christianity. Pray, pray, pray. I am speaking to myself, as well. I don't pray enough, but I am always working on improving this discipline. This is why Jesus gave me The Four Commands of Christ. These are His words, not mine. Listen to them.

In the morning, LORD, you hear my voice; in the morning I lay my requests before you and wait expectantly. (Psalm 5:3)

Come, let us bow down in worship, let us kneel before the LORD our Maker. (Psalm 95:6)

I rise before dawn and cry for help; I have put my hope in your word. (Psalm 119:147)

"As surely as I live," says the Lord, "every knee will bow before me; every tongue will acknowledge God." (Romans 14:11)

Three times a day he got down on his knees and prayed, giving thanks to his God, just as he had done before. (Daniel 6:10)

...for this reason, I bow my knees before the Father. (Ephesians 3:14)

Praying has been a practice throughout history. If you look at the men who made prayer a main part of their daily life, the ones who started their day on their knees, you see the likes of King David, Daniel, and many more. So why don't we do this in our own lives? If prayer can get the attention of Jesus and faith as small as a mustard seed can move mountains, why aren't we spending more time with Jesus? Let's get going and move mountains of blessing due to the world. Let's loose the Holy Spirit to work wonders for His glory. If it weren't for the present times and distractions, we probably would be praying more. So, make prayer a front and center governing value to glorify God.

God is always working toward saving us from ourselves, and He never changes. He is the same today as He always has been. What would happen if you would gather with some Christian buddies and start praying for your hometown? Pray for revival. Pray for some individual to accept Christ. Miracles can happen if we pray: people can be healed, people can be born again, relationships and marriages can be reconciled. Wow, if we would only pray! Some of you will submit, and some of you will not. For those of you who are willing to submit, start by getting on your knees every morning when you roll out of bed and pray to God. Show Him that you are willing to start your day by humbling yourself and submitting to His authority here on earth as it is in heaven.[53] When you are on your knees, adopt the attitude of the sinful woman with the alabaster jar that covered Jesus's feet.

When a sinful woman from that town learned that Jesus was dining there, she brought an alabaster jar of perfume. As she stood behind Him at His feet weeping, she began to wet His feet with her tears and wipe them with her hair. Then she kissed His feet and anointed them with the perfume. When the Pharisee who had invited Jesus saw this, he said to himself, "If this man were a prophet, He would know who this is and what kind of woman is touching Him—for she is a sinner!" And Jesus answered him, "Simon, I have something to say to you." And he replied, "Say it, Teacher." He said,

---

53 Matthew 6:10

"A moneylender had two debtors: one owed five hundred denarii, and the other fifty. When they were unable to repay, he graciously forgave them both. So, which of them will love him more?" Simon answered and said, "I suppose the one whom he forgave more." And He said to him, "You have judged correctly." Turning toward the woman, He said to Simon, "Do you see this woman? I entered your house; you gave Me no water for My feet, but she has wet My feet with her tears and wiped them with her hair. You gave Me no kiss; but she, since the time I came in, has not ceased to kiss My feet. You did not anoint My head with oil, but she anointed My feet with perfume. For this reason, I say to you, her sins, which are many, have been forgiven, for she loved much; but he who is forgiven little, loves little." Then He said to her, "Your sins have been forgiven." Those who were reclining at the table with Him began to say to themselves, "Who is this man who even forgives sins?" And He said to the woman, "Your faith has saved you; go in peace." (Luke 7:37-50)

I used this Scripture to give you an idea of the attitude you should have when you are on your knees praying. It is important to start on your knees because it is an expression of the First Command of Christ to humble yourself and submit. When I am on my knees praying, I come to realize all of my sins and acknowledge what Jesus has forgiven. I then move forward with intercessory prayer, requests, share with God plans for the future, and thankfulness.

When I was twenty-six years old, I partnered with four gentlemen to finance a large development project my company was working on. About two years into our venture, I accepted Jesus into my heart. One of the men remarked that I seemed different and asked what had changed. I told them that I had accepted Jesus into my heart but didn't know what to do with it. It felt similar to when I was sixteen years old and first accepted Christ in my heart but didn't know how to live it. I was confused and had not been anchored by my previous church. These men tried to help me with church advice for new Christians, but I couldn't quite wrap my head around some of their concepts. These men were trying to indoctrinate me into a religion that baptized the dead into heaven, which just didn't seem possible to me. I prayed about it and asked God to help me with the real answer. A short time afterward, I went to visit my sister and attended church with her.

At the door greeting people was a tall, redheaded preacher. I am a man of good size myself, but he was two inches taller than me and had a strong voice. I thought I would ask him about the church and this doctrine my business partners had talked to me about. When the preacher shook my hand, I asked him the question, "What do you know about baptizing the dead into Heaven?"

He replied, "Just listen to the sermon today and you will know the answer to that question." I was stunned. I couldn't believe my ears! How could he know what question I was going to ask? Jesus knew. He knows what we need and when we need it.

He preached on the story of the rich man and Lazarus. When the preacher started talking about the deep chasm between heaven and hell that cannot be crossed, I knew he had answered the question of my heart. Without a doubt, Jesus answered my heartfelt question that I had prayed for days about. He did not leave me emptyhanded; I knew what I needed to do.

Just as the story of the rich man and Lazarus warns against living large, what will we decide to do? How will we accept the truth of the Bible and live out our life? This decision we make will determine whether we go to heaven or hell. This is why I am pleading through this book for all of you to choose this day your destination. Accept Jesus as your savior and live in Heaven forever.

But if serving the LORD seems undesirable to you, then choose for yourselves this day whom you will serve, whether the gods your ancestors served beyond the Euphrates, or the gods of the

Amorites, in whose land you are living. But as for me and my household, we will serve the LORD. (Joshua 24:15)

Choosing to accept Jesus into your heart is life. I know your first reaction is to exit this environment of speaking truth and run. I just want you to know that if you continue rejecting Jesus's calling, then you have chosen death by default. In the Garden of Eden after Adam and Eve sinned, they too fled at the presence of God. Jesus's light is so bright that the lost turn away from it. Darkness flees from it. Please, turn into the light by accepting Jesus as your Savior and Lord.

Whoever believes and is baptized will be saved, but whoever does not believe will be condemned. (Mark 16:16)

This is the confidence we have in approaching God: that if we ask anything according to his will, he hears us. (1 John 5:14 NASB)

I believe Christ gives you whatever you ask in the spiritual sense. Not what will cause you to fall—like a million dollars or a new car—but what will give you victory over the Satan-led world. His will for us is to love Him with all we have and to love others as ourselves. Jesus said He has overcome the world but not so we could enrich ourselves. Spend time with God and you will succeed as a Christian. Use this to start praying over the lost, praying over the sick, praying over the lame, praying for your friends. Jesus stated, *"Very truly I tell you, whoever believes in me will do the works I have been doing, and they will do even greater things than these because I am going to the Father"* (John 14:12). Our prayers will be answered and will move mountains, if we stay in His will.

One day, I was praying and began to imagine that I was in the Pharisee's house when Mary was anointing Jesus's feet. I imagined that my tears were washing His feet, and I was anointing His feet with perfume (the perfume is my prayers). The sense of being in His presence was overwhelming. After that experience, I felt humbled when I prayed.

Continuously pray to Jesus, King of Kings, Lord of Lords. He is our all, and to Him we give our all. He created in us an all-consuming fire, *fuego*.

Chapter 8

Read Your Bible

"Jesus answered, 'It is written: 'Man shall not live on bread alone, but on every word that comes from the mouth of God.'"

Matthew 4:4

Reading your Bible provides the architecture of your life. It is the link between you and God. You will find life everlasting there. You will find all the answers that your heart desires. You will find solace. You will find how to live and how to behave. You will find peace, not as the world gives but only as God can give you through His Word.

Your word is a lamp for my feet, a light on my path. (Psalm 119:105)

All Scripture is God-breathed and is useful for teaching, rebuking, correcting and training in righteousness, so that the servant of God may be thoroughly equipped for every good work. (2 Timothy 3:16-17)

God's word is living and active, but not in the sense that you can change God's word to bend to political correctness in these current times. What God says in the Bible is how it is, period. All the stories used in the Bible are intended to teach all of us valuable lessons. They also give us insight into actions to take for Him such as the Fourth Command of Christ.

> *For the word of God is alive and active. Sharper than any double-edged sword, it penetrates even to dividing soul and spirit, joints and marrow; it judges the thoughts and attitudes of the heart. (Hebrews 4:12)*

> *Do not conform to the pattern of this world but be transformed by the renewing of your mind. Then you will be able to test and approve what God's will is—his good, pleasing and perfect will. (Romans 12:2)*

How do you renew your mind? Only by reading the Bible. You need to fill all your extra time with good Christian activities, music, videos, and literature.

> *The eye is the lamp of our body. What we view through our eyes can defile us or bring light to us. What we are taught throughout the years can define us. Train a child in the way they should go and they will never depart from it. (Proverbs 22:6)*

It is important that we see the light while we can. Do not let yourself be deceived into believing that we have evolved, and we are no longer in need of a higher authority. We need Jesus in our lives so much so that we need to submit our all to Him.

> *While it is daytime, we must do the works of Him who sent Me. Night is coming, when no one can work. While I am in the world, I am the light of the world. (John 9:4-5)*

If you continuously read the Bible, while you can, Jesus will open your mind to truth. He says, "If you seek after me as if you are seeking silver and gold, I will reveal Myself to you." [54]

Then he opened their minds so they could understand the Scriptures. (Luke 24:45)

Let the message of Christ dwell among you richly as you teach and admonish one another with all wisdom through psalms, hymns, and songs from the Spirit, singing to God with gratitude in your hearts. (Colossians 3:16)

Until I come, devote yourself to the public reading of Scripture, to preaching and to teaching. (1 Timothy 4:13)

My son, if you accept my words and hide my commandments within you, if you incline your ear to wisdom and direct your heart to understanding, if you truly call out to insight and lift your voice to understanding, if you seek it like silver and search it out like hidden treasure, then you will discern the fear of the LORD and discover the knowledge of God. (Proverbs 2:1-5)

In the beginning was the Word, and the Word was with God, and the Word was God. He was with God in the beginning. Through him all things were made; without him nothing was made that has been made. In him was life, and that life was the light of all mankind. The light shines in the darkness, and the darkness has not overcome it. (John 1:1-5)

54 Proverbs 2

Therefore everyone who hears these words of mine and puts them into practice is like a wise man who built his house on the rock. (Matthew 7:24)

God says we need to read our Bible first thing in the morning and last thing at night. God cannot communicate with you if you do not read the Bible. It is the gateway to heaven, if you follow its decrees. It is the straight and narrow way. It is *life*. Give Jesus a chance to change your life and your relationship with Him by reading the Bible and praying.

Chapter 9

Memorize Scripture

"Keep this Book of the Law always on your lips; meditate on it day and night, so that you may be careful to do everything written in it. Then you will be prosperous and successful."

Joshua 1:8

Why are we to memorize Scripture? When Jesus was tempted by Satan at the end of his forty days and forty nights of fasting in the desert, He answered His accuser using Scripture. Now, I know He wrote all of Scripture, but He was teaching us a point here: Use Scripture to reject and overcome sin. Use Scripture as your basis and standard. In our modern world, we are faced with questions like whether we should see a movie knowing it has bad language or nudity. If you memorized Scripture, you would know that your eyes are the entrance to your heart. Even Job said he had not allowed his eye to venture toward young maidens.[55]

We need a strong Biblical base to keep us centered on Christ, and we build that base by knowing Scripture. Here is some Scripture to start your memorization program:

---

55 Job 31:1

How can a young person stay on the path of purity? By living according to your word. (Psalm 119:9)

The law of their God is in their hearts; their feet do not slip. (Psalm 37:31)

Bind them always on your heart; fasten them around your neck. When you walk, they will guide you; when you sleep, they will watch over you; when you awake, they will speak to you. (Proverbs 6:21-22)

I have stored up your word in my heart, that I might not sin against you. (Psalm 119:11)

Memorizing Scripture will help you have victory over sin. When your body is telling you to do this or do that, then your heart, mind, and soul can remind you why you shouldn't and can help you state to Satan why you will not. Christ used Scripture to thwart Satan's temptations. Jesus quoted from Isaiah for all the temptations Satan put before Him. When the temptations were over, Satan was forced to flee. He did not have permission to go further. The fallen angels will also flee at the written Word when used correctly in Christ's name. I learned long ago to place a hedge of protection[56] around me and my loved ones and bind[57] Satan in the name of Jesus.

What shall we say then? Shall we continue in sin, that grace may abound? God forbid. How shall we, that are dead to sin, live any longer therein? Know ye not, that so many of us as were baptized into Jesus Christ were baptized into his death? Therefore, we are buried with him by baptism into

---

56 Job 1:10
57 Matthew 18:18

*death: that like as Christ was raised up from the dead by the
glory of the Father, even so we also should walk in newness
of life. (Romans 6:1-7 KJV)*

There is power in Christ over the spiritual realm that affects us here
on earth. The lame are made to walk again, the deaf to speak again. Evil
spirits are removed and thrown out to the unknown. If you are lost or just
are not sure about which direction you should take, then get your bearings
by praying to Jesus and asking the questions you have in your heart.

Have you ever been in a spot where someone wants to make a point
using Scripture, but somehow it doesn't seem right? Some people will
take Scripture and twist it to their own desired outcome. If you are not
anchored in Christ, you may be swayed.

I knew an older gentleman who was born into a Christian family
and went to church his whole life. He taught Sunday school and
participated in weekly Bible studies but never groomed his personal
relationship with Christ. When he became older and was confined
to a care center, unable to attend his church, he became interested in
other religions and was swayed by a non-Christian faith. He went to
church all his life, but he never memorized Scripture or committed
himself to Jesus entirely.

Is that you? Have you been to church all your life but never
actually bought in to Christ by humbling yourself and asking Jesus
into your life? What is your method of maintaining your relationship
with Christ? By applying yourself to the Four Commands of Christ
and the expressions of faith, you will maintain that relationship with
Christ. When we memorize Scripture, the Bible says, *"All Scripture
is God-breathed and is useful for teaching, rebuking, correcting and
training in righteousness, so that the servant of God may be thoroughly
equipped for every good work"* (2 Timothy 3: 16-17).

Memory-forming can become a healthy lifelong habit. Researchers
from the National Institute on Health and Aging have found that adults
who went through short bursts of memory training were better able to
maintain higher cognitive functioning and everyday skills, even five
years after going through the training. Practicing memorization allowed

the elderly adults to delay typical cognitive decline by seven to fourteen years. Students who start practicing memory training now can stay sharp in years to come. [58] Exercise your brain. Good mental health helps you cope with life as it happens to you. Good mental health will leave you with inner peace and a sense of well-being. Just as you take care of your body, you need to take care of your mind.

Chuck Swindoll wrote, "I know of no other single practice in the Christian life more rewarding, practically speaking, than memorizing scripture… your mind will become alert and observant."[59]

It is by memorization and reading your Bible that you are able to stave off sin (see Psalms 119:9-16, Jeremiah 15:16, Proverbs 3:3, Joshua 1:8, and Psalms 37:31).

Fix these words of mine in your hearts and minds; tie them as symbols on your hands and bind them on your foreheads. (Deuteronomy 11:18)

Jesus answered, "It is written: 'Man shall not live on bread alone, but on every word that comes from the mouth of God.'" (Matthew 4:4)

My son, be attentive to my words; incline your ear to my sayings. Let them not escape from your sight; keep them within your heart." (Proverbs 4:20-21 ESV)

I have not departed from the commandment of his lips; I have treasured the words of his mouth more than my portion of food. (Job 23:12 ESV)

---

58 https://www.brainscape.com/blog/2012/07/memorization-brain-benefits/
59 Taken from Growing Strong in the Seasons of Life by Charles R. Swindoll. Copyright © 1983, 1994, 2007 by Charles R. Swindoll. Used by permission of HarperCollins Christian Publishing. www.harpercollinschristian.com

There are many reasons to memorize Scripture. I have laid out a few: to improve mental health and mental clarity, to stave off sin pressures, to correct others, to know the truth, and to cultivate character. Try memorizing one set of Scripture per week. Write the Scripture on a three-by-five notecard and practice it all week, then repeat it to a friend or your spouse and move on to the next. Memorization is a deeply rewarding practice. Start today and notice the positive benefits it has on your life.

Chapter 10

Tithe Your Money

"A tithe of everything from the land, whether grain from the soil or fruit from the trees, belongs to the LORD; it is holy to the LORD... Every tithe of the herd and flock—every tenth animal that passes under the shepherd's rod—will be holy to the LORD."

Leviticus 27:30-32

Tithing, which translates to "tenth" in Hebrew and means to offer one-tenth of your income, is an old tradition to keep God's messengers in the black financially. God instructed Israel to tithe as a means to keep the priests monetarily supported. Everyone on earth needs to eat, sleep, and have a roof over their head. There hasn't always been a welfare agency to take care of us.

If you are unwilling to tithe, how can God answer your prayers? How can you rob God and still expect Him to answer your prayers? God is slow to anger and very gracious, so He will probably answer your prayer anyway because He loves us so much. But how can you be in the zone?

Tithing is the beginning of your faith. All of us at one time or another have lacked faith to tithe. Our excuse is we need the money to survive and pay our bills because we are living paycheck to paycheck. Sound familiar? What patience He has for all who don't tithe. When you are working out your salvation in Christ and you leave these important, absolute truths out of your spiritual formation plan, then the destroyer is able to invade your space. You need to put on the full armor of God, and tithing is a part of that.

> *"Because I, the LORD, do not change, you descendants of Jacob have not been destroyed. Yet from the days of your fathers, you have turned away from My statutes and have not kept them. Return to Me, and I will return to you," says the LORD of Hosts. "But you ask, 'How can we return?' Will a man rob God? Yet you are robbing Me! But you ask, 'How do we rob You?' In tithes and offerings. You are cursed with a curse, yet you—the whole nation—are still robbing Me. Bring the full tithe into the storehouse, so that there may be food in My house. Test Me in this," says the LORD of Hosts. "See if I will not open the windows of heaven and pour out for you blessing without measure. I will rebuke the devourer for you, so that it will not destroy the fruits of your land, and the vine in your field will not fail to produce fruit," says the LORD of Hosts. (Malachi 3:6-11)*

I agree with the preachers I have known throughout my life who say that your tithe should be the first check you write each month. Honor God with your money, and He will honor you. They received their knowledge of this from the Bible. In Genesis 4:3-5, we read how the first fruit was to be dedicated to the Lord. And in Leviticus 23:10, the Lord instructed the Israelites to bring a sheaf of their first grain to the priest.

I once made an extra $3,000 when I had little money to my name but after praying about how to spend the money I used it according to my prayer. Wouldn't you know, a surprise medical bill came due, which left me strapped. I have to admit that I was a little nervous, but I prayed, and my prayer was, "Not my will, but thine." I knew, though, in my heart He would come through. Lo and behold, I received a phone call from someone who owed me a large sum of money saying they had just put a check in the mail. Praise the Lord. Promise made, promise kept.

We all must put our most treasured you-name-it on the altar as Abraham did with Isaac in Genesis 22:1-17 because, when we do, God answers in marvelous ways. If you don't put it all on the altar, then you are robbing yourself of the great miracles God does for us and the stories that could come out of these miracles. God has even enjoined us to test Him here. Where have you ever heard of God saying, "Test me?" I always had the mindset not to test the Lord: *"Do not put the LORD your God to the test as you did at Massah"* (Deuteronomy 6:16). In every way, the Bible tells us not to test our God, yet God himself tell us to test Him in this one discipline: tithing. It seems reasonable to me that we should listen, and we should pay our tithe.

So, how do you start paying tithe from scratch? Start with prayer. Tell God you are going to tithe but need to get your budget in order. In some ways, you are making a deal with God. You need to quit living off of God's 10 percent. Adjust your budget and cut back on anything that is not an absolute necessity and start tithing at the same time. Make the commitment and actually tithe. Take it from your account first so you can't renege later on. Then learn what to dump in your budget all at the same time. I am not saying it will be easy; I am saying trust God. Trust that if He feeds the sparrow, He will feed us, and he will clothe us. This is called faith.

In the same way that we love our own children, God has the same feelings toward us. I have had moments where I suddenly start crying because I miss my sons who are grown and living in different states, even though I am one to mostly cover up my emotions. He loved us from the moment that He placed His spirit seed in our mother's womb. We are His children, and He is our father. He cries inside for all the people who are walking away from Him. Can we not begin to obey our father in heaven by paying our tithe? Give Him back what He desires from us to show our love to Him. He never fails.

In one of my real estate classes, the instructor taught that we should pay our taxes, pay our tithe, put 10 percent in savings, and live off the rest. I think this is a good plan. I know we have children and bills that need to be paid, but God does say to test Him in this. If you pay your tithe first before any other bill, then you will be forced to live off the rest. Trust God because something will happen to make your budget work out. Satan will also use this opportunity to kill and destroy your new faith challenge in God. Satan's job is to steal from you the promises of God. Satan is the father of all lies and will make your life miserable for serving the King of Kings. Trust and faith in God will overcome if you do not waver.

Tithing is a discipline in faith. Without faith, we will not be saved or see Jesus. Someday, our faith will be challenged. The testing of our faith is a normal Christian process. Each of us receives hardships at some point in our life. We can overcome all of this by starting our day off on our knees and asking God to be a part of everything that we are. Put it all on the altar. Let Jesus fight your battle, even your monetary battle. You know why? He has already won; you just need to realize it and live it. Let this be our prayer:

> *Jesus, we will pay our tithe today, so give us grace and mercy to see us through this. After all, Jesus, this is your money that I am just managing. Help me to be a better manager, and I will always put you first. Protect me from the evil one as I walk this narrow path of Yours.*

What are churches for anyway? Are they not for our benefit in the long run? Churches need money to pay the bills and especially to pay the pastoral staff and any team they have put together to minister. Churches are there for the continuance of Christ's teaching. He completed His message to us humans on earth through His apostles and Paul. Someone has to keep us pumped up and headed in the right direction. Some of you only hear God's Word on Sundays because you feel you are too busy to read the Bible. We need to change this, and maybe the paying of your tithe will change this attitude.

If you are still struggling with tithing, I suggest going to your elders or pastor and discussing this important issue with them. They may have a better plan of transition. Personal finance expert Dave Ramsey has helpful discussions about tithing on his blog.[60] He also has good advice on how to balance a budget, manage finances, and get out of debt. God wants us to be free of the slavery of debt; be wise in your financial decisions and seek out advice when you need it.

> *Remember this: Whoever sows sparingly will also reap sparingly, and whoever sows generously will also reap generously. Each one should give what he has decided in his heart to give, not out of regret or compulsion. For God loves a cheerful giver. And God is able to make all grace abound to you, so that in all things, at all times, having all that you need, you will abound in every good work.*
> *(2 Corinthians 9:6-8)*

We must give according to what we feel God is asking; at a minimum, I tithe 10 percent of my income. We need to be careful that when we give, we give faithfully and cheerfully. Do not let anyone compel you to give. I have heard of some churches pushing their congregation to give all they have. I say pay only what the Holy Spirit tells you to pay. If you are thinking of giving large sums to a religious organization, please consult with an attorney, a financial consultant, your friends, and of course your pastor if you have one. I am not saying don't give; I am saying to know all of your options and seek out advice from trusted people.

I would like everyone to tithe and pay it first before anything else. When you see God holding up His end, you will be so joyful that you will overflow with joy. Developing a habit of paying tithe will also help you years down the road when you or someone else is having financial trouble for whatever reason. You will pull from the experience of God providing for you and can in turn give them advice with confidence.

---

60 https://www.daveramsey.com/blog/daves-advice-on-tithing-and-giving

You can also hold someone else's hand and give them confidence that God will see them through the trouble.

Finances are one of the leading causes of divorce among Christians and non-Christians alike. If we can use God's method for finances, then this discipline could save families. Put God to the test, as He says in Malachi. Let Him show you His love for you. Have Faith in Jesus.

Chapter 11

Tithe Your Time

"Look carefully then how you walk, not as unwise but as wise, making the best use of the time, because the days are evil. Therefore do not be foolish, but understand what the will of the Lord is."

Ephesians 5:15-17

Even though the word "tithe" is not used in relation to time in the Bible, there are many passages about needing to spend time with God. After all, isn't time the main ingredient in our relationship with God? When we pray and memorize Scripture, are we not, in a sense, tithing our time? Not spending time with God will cause separation in our relationship with Him. Just because this spiritual discipline is not written in the Bible does not mean it is unimportant and should be disregarded.

God knows you and what you are capable of handling in your life. Deuteronomy says to love the Lord with all your strength and might, but are we doing that? We are at odds with ourselves when it comes to spending time with God. We know we should, but the busyness of life keeps us away from reading our Bible and praying. We have too many distractions in our lives that we have ascribed more importance to. Maybe we think we have plenty of time to get our relationship with

God right, and we just need to focus our time on building wealth for a little longer. What has all the time spent on acquiring stuff given us? Peace? No. Tranquility? No. Fullness of life? No. Health? No. Joy? No. Spending time with God will give you all of the above and abundantly.

With the Four Commands of Christ, God has made it easier than ever to live faithfully with Him. I may be repeating myself, but I need to so this concept will sink in. God makes this clear in Deuteronomy:

> *This day I call the heavens and the earth as witnesses*
> *against you that I have set before you, life and death,*
> *blessings and curses. Now choose life, so that you and your*
> *children may live and that you may love the* LORD *your*
> *God, listen to his voice, and hold fast to him. (Deuteronomy*
> *30:19-20)*

How can you say you love the Lord your God with all your heart, with all your soul, and with all your mind without spending quality time with Him? We determine how we spend our time. I am trying to warn everyone, including myself, that we need to spend more time with God than we think we should. If you are tithing your time to God, then Hallelujah; if not, make a paradigm change in your life and make it a goal to set aside more time for God. You will never regret it.

One way to make that paradigm shift is to explore your governing values, the things that are most important to you in life that guide how you spend your money, time, and energy. Governing values will help us to sort out our goals in life and why we are here. What are the goals you have in mind for your life? Is God at the center of these goals? Or is it money, possessions, adventures, sport? What drives you to spend so much time, energy, and effort on those endeavors that you choose over God? Maybe the answer is that we Christians are not fulfilling our role as teachers of Christ, expressing the goodness of God and the marvelous benefits of being in a relationship with Jesus. We also should teach what life is without Jesus being at the center of it. God has set up rules for us to follow, rules to keep us on the road to success. He has also stated that these rules come at a high price, and few find it. That high price is your time. He tells us that we will find life everlasting when we follow His commands: *"If you love Me, you will keep My commandments"* (John 14:15).

In order to keep His commandments, you need to know what they are first, which means spend timing with the Bible. How will you teach your children about God if you don't read to them about God's love? Having them recite Scripture will take time, too. If you follow the Four Commands of Christ and set aside the First Command, then you will spend time getting to know the Father better and better. Your relationship with God is about spending time with Him.

Should we tithe ten percent of our time like we tithe ten percent of our money? I believe that spending 2.4 hours a day with God would make a positive change in our lives and especially in our relationship with God and is a good goal to have. If we want to take spending time with God seriously, then let us start setting goals in that direction. Take a piece of paper and write "Goal-Setting Plan" at the top. Below it, create a schedule for your week. Each day, set aside ten minutes for prayer followed by ten minutes of reading the Bible. The next week, set aside fifteen minutes for prayer and reading. Continue this until you reach 2.4 hours a day. You may want to include other disciplines, but don't do too many at a time; you don't want to overload yourself with too much on your plate. It may take you a year or two to reach your goal, but it will be worth it. Why do you want write this down? Goals are a wish until you write them down. If you write your goals down and journal daily, you will find a very happy change in your life. Any movement toward God will bring everlasting reward.

Chapter 12

Thank God Always

"God loves a cheerful giver."

2 Corinthians 9:7

T hank God for all the blessings that He has bestowed upon you. Thank Him because you are alive in a time where our health—and quite frankly every aspect of life—is better than it has ever been in the history of the world. Thank Him because He loved you so much that He gave the ultimate sacrifice for you and me. He has saved us from eternal death *if* we choose to have a relationship with Him.

> *Whoever has ears, let them hear what the Spirit says to the churches. To the one who is victorious, I will give the right to eat from the tree of life, which is in the paradise of God. (Revelation 2:7)*
>
> *Enter His gates with thanksgiving and His courts with praise; give thanks to Him and bless His name.* (Psalm 100:4)

How will you become victorious? He has given us a way. Thank the Lord with all your might, with all your strength, with all your mind, and with all your soul. I thank God for everything many times. I thank Him for my children and my grandchildren. I thank Him for my job. I thank Him for my health even though I have cancer. I thank Him because no matter what condition I am in, it could always be worse. Now, I have to admit I am not thankful right away for bad things that happen to me. Like most of you, I start with, "Why did you let this happen to me? Why did you not reveal to me that this was going to happen to me? If you would have, I would have prepared myself mentally and be ready for it!"

I once knew a woman who blamed God for twenty years for the death of her infant baby. It took an evangelist specializing in freeing people from bitterness to help free her from guilt and blame. And when Jesus frees you, you are free indeed. Boy, was she on fire after the chains were broken and fell off of her. This seems to be a constant in all of us humans, blaming God for all the bad things that happen to us or losing belief in God when something shakes at our foundation. When I have that attitude, I am reminded by the Holy Spirit of the Parable of the Weeds.

> *Jesus put before them another parable: "The kingdom of heaven is like a man who sowed good seed in his field, but while everyone was asleep, his enemy came and sowed weeds among the wheat, and slipped away. When the wheat sprouted and bore grain, then the weeds also appeared. The owner's servants came to him and said, 'Sir, didn't you sow good seed in your field? Where then did the weeds come from?' 'An enemy did this,' he replied. So, the servants asked him, 'Do you want us to go and pull them up?' 'No,' he said, 'if you pull the weeds now, you might uproot the wheat with them. Let both grow together until the harvest. At that time, I will tell the harvesters: First collect the weeds and tie them in bundles to be burned; then gather the wheat into my barn." (Matthew 13:24-30)*

What does this mean? It means that Satan is alive and well and continues to work at destroying us Christians. Jesus won't remove the bad on this earth without causing harm to the good. Do not think our lives on earth will be free of issues or problems. God has set the earth and the universe in motion, and it will go where it is designed to go. The universe has its own way of healing and keeping nature in balance. When our universe gets turned upside down, we need to be in a close relationship with Christ. He can soothe our soul as we go through the good and the bad along this path that we call life.

When I am handling grievances, sorrows, and misfortunes, I first go to Him in prayer and ask for understanding of why certain things happen to me and how I should overcome it. Most of the time, it's me. I have a sin or an issue between me and God that I did not clear up and needs attention. It could also be that God is allowing this to happen to help me mature. God is God, and He is sovereign. Satan cannot control who I am, and he cannot control my belief in Jesus. I don't always start out with an attitude of thankfulness because of my sin nature. I seem to let my feelings show before I am able to wrap myself around God's love for me. So, my sin nature says to God, "Why did you let that happen to me?" But my spiritual nature eventually says, "It is well with my soul."

I often look to the Book of Job for answers. Job was a man who must have been remarkably close to God, because God allowed Satan to test him. Satan told God the only reason Job loved Him was because he'd been blessed with riches and wagered that Job would curse God if all of his wealth was taken away. God told Satan to do what he wanted apart from killing him. Satan destroyed all that Job owned, even killing Job's children.

> *Then Job's wife said to him, "Do you still retain your integrity? Curse God and die!" "You speak as a foolish woman speaks," he told her. "Should we accept from God only good and not adversity?" In all this, Job did not sin in what he said. Job did not sin by charging God with wrongdoing. (Job 2:9-10)*

God did not let all these calamities happen to Job because he had sinned; He allowed the calamities to happen because Job was blameless before God. Job's story teaches us how we should respond when something bad happens to us. It also teaches us that Satan cannot touch us without God's permission. We are all God's servants, and He has the right to mold us any way He chooses. We must maintain an attitude that "it is well with my soul."

Praising God is being thankful, and it is worship. Remember, your purpose in life is to glorify God. One way to glorify God is to always be thankful. Some may say, "How is God glorified in my pain? How is God glorified by the way people treat me? How can I be thankful when I just can't seem to get a break?" He is glorified when you give Him your pain. He is also glorified in the way that you surrender yourself even when you are in a negative situation. He is glorified by the way you thank the Lord even though the pain seems beyond a person's ability to manage at the time.

Remember, *"God loves a cheerful giver"* (2 Corinthians 9:7). Be cheerful in *all* your ways. Our circumstances could always be worse! What if your life was taken and you had to go before the judgment seat with a heavy heart against the Lord? Don't be like the ten lepers who were healed by Jesus. There were ten healed, but only one came back to thank Him. What did Jesus say to that one lone leper? *"Then he said to him, 'Rise and go; your faith has made you well'"* (Luke 17:19). Jesus called the leper's thankfulness "faith." Faith is a form of worship, is it not? Without faith, can you even believe in Jesus? Without faith, can you move a mountain? Without thankfulness, can you really have a relationship with God? Examine yourself and see if you are thankful (faithful).

> *Now on his way to Jerusalem, Jesus traveled along the border between Samaria and Galilee. As he was going into a village, ten men who had leprosy met him. They stood at a distance and called out in a loud voice, "Jesus, Master, have pity on us!" When he saw them, he said, "Go, show your-selves to the priests." And as they went, they were cleansed. One of them, when he saw he was healed, came back,*

praising God in a loud voice. He threw himself at Jesus's feet and thanked him—and he was a Samaritan. Jesus asked, "Were not all ten cleansed? Where are the other nine? Has no one returned to give praise to God except this for-eigner?" Then he said to him, "Rise and go; your faith has made you well." (Luke 17: 11-19)

While the other nine lepers were physically healed, their relationship to God was not healed. The tenth leper was healed inside and out because He praised God and went back to thank Jesus for his cleansing. If we thank the Lord for our grievances, will we not be healed? Will not Jesus set our hearts free from the pain that we feel? Yes, He will set you free. This does not mean you will not feel the sorrow and pain of the situation, but you will have a joy in your heart and a peace that is beyond understanding. I try to tell new Christians that we all will feel pain, whether it is the pain of an unfaithful partner or the pain of a lost child or health issues. Jesus fills the void that we feel as we go through our pain and fills us with His love. We can never lose sight of the fact that it happened, but we know that Christ doesn't allow anything to happen to us that is not beneficial to us, one way or another.

These are the times we need to find things to be thankful for: friend-ships, family, sharing the gospel. How does Jesus help us with the pain? When we give it to Him on the altar and refocus, He comes and brings peace. I call this *Shalom Adonai*. Ask Jesus to help you with your pain. Get involved with your church and mentor someone; this always will take your mind off of your situation. Ask Jesus to help tender your heart toward Him so you can see the peace that He pursues you with.

Thankfulness unto the Lord was shown in the Old Testament by what is called a peace offering or a fellowship offering.

Now this is the law of the sacrifice of peace offerings which shall be presented to the LORD. If he offers it by way of thanksgiving, then along with the sacrifice of thanksgiving he shall offer unleavened cakes mixed with oil, and unleavened wafers spread with oil, and cakes of well-stirred fine flour mixed with oil. (Leviticus 7:11-12)

When you sacrifice a fellowship offering to the LORD, sacrifice it in such a way that it will be accepted on your behalf. (Leviticus 19:5)

Offer your thankfulness to the Lord with a glad heart, and you will be healed, physically and mentally. Thankfulness is faith, and by faith are you healed.[61]

Now, I must also say that you can be thankful and full of faith and still not be healed from your grievance or infirmity. When Paul asked God many times to be healed from the thorn in his flesh, Jesus said, *"But He said to me, 'My grace is sufficient for you, for My power is perfected in weakness'"* (2 Corinthians 12:9). I do not want to make everyone think that faith is all that is needed to be healed. This subject can be complicated and confusing because it is up to Jesus to determine when and whether a person will be healed. Remember, God's plan transcends our understanding, and sometimes, Jesus does not reveal it to us. We have to move in faith and let it be a major part of our worship. We may not be healed from our grievances, but there is always a divine reason. We live with whatever God gives us to live with, and we thank Him for it. As I have said before , it could always be worse.

Love the Lord with all your heart, mind, and soul, no matter your circumstance or situation. There is always a reason for what God allows in our lives. Let us all be thankful to the Lord every minute of our lives. I really do mean every minute. Don't let apathy steal your joy. Instead, take the attitude that it is well with your soul and always thank God. Thank Him for all that He has given us. Be thankful.

---

61 Mark 10:52

Chapter 13

Fasting

"Is not this the kind of fasting I have chosen: to lose the chains of injustice and untie the cords of the yoke, to set the oppressed free and break every yoke?"

Isaiah 58: 6

Where does fasting come from, and why do we use it in Christianity? Fasting has been around for at least 4,000 years. There are several ancient texts that describe the use of fasting as a means of healing yourself. God loves for us to use it for our spiritual formation.

Fasting is the practice of giving up food and possibly water for a certain amount of time to achieve a spiritual goal. I always recommend that the reason for the fast or the spiritual goal should be written down, and the results should be documented. This will help you to know how God answered you and to share Christ with others. I guarantee you that, several days or weeks later, Satan will say, "Did God *really* answer that prayer?" If you have your results written down, then you will know exactly how to respond.

Fasting can be physically cleansing; however, fasting may not be appropriate for everyone and can have a dark side for those who are underprepared. Some are not capable of fasting due to physical conditions. For example, I have diabetes, so I have to be careful when I fast. My suggestion is do not even consider a fast until you have worked it out with your doctor to make sure it is safe for you. I also do not support fasting without water. I normally do a three-day fast with water as needed. However you decide to fast, just make sure you approach it in a healthy way and talk to your doctor first.

So, why do we fast? The question is incredibly important as our fast is anchored by the intent we bring to it. Is it for a closer relationship with God? Or for an answer to a specific prayer request? Try to be specific each time you fast, and don't have multiple goals. And don't forget to pray when you fast; fasting and praying go hand in hand, like peanut butter and jelly. Here are ten potential goals that can be supported with fasting:

- When you feel you want a closeness to Christ without any other reason. The duration of this fast should come from an agreement between you and God.

- When you need an answer from God. Maybe God has already given the answer or direction in your heart, but you just don't believe it. This is when you need to fast to clarify how God is directing you.

- When you want to start a new work in your ministry. When you fast for these kinds of issues, you should fast personally and possibly corporately (with others). Always use your fast to glorify God. Then wait on God for His answers.

- When you feel you need a change of direction. For this goal, it's especially important to have a timeframe. Absent this level of detail, you can get derailed. Start with attainable goals, then work toward them. Never promise or dedicate a fast to God. [62]

---

62 James 5:12

Leave room and be open to God should He ask of you something different.

• When you want to engage in spiritual warfare. There are a lot of lost people, even people who are close to us, and we need to fast and pray for those lost souls who are bound by evil spirits. Some barriers, or strongholds as Jesus says, will only be broken down by fasting and prayer.[63] Fasting is an offensive weapon when you have to put on the full armor of God.

• When you get some awful news, you know of a situation that entangles your mind, or maybe your church needs answers. Consider calling for a holy fast of the congregation.[64]

• When you have committed a sin and you want to repent from it. Humble yourself and pray, and God will answer your prayer. King David wrote about his sin with Bathsheba, which resulted in a beautiful prayer.[65] It doesn't hurt to recite this prayer for yourself, too. Fasting and praying gets God's attention.

• When disaster hits, including fatal accidents, famines, earthquakes, floods, hurricanes, and tsunamis. The end times are upon us, and we are in labor pains; if we lose our freedom to worship or are persecuted to the point of being fed to the lions, should we not humble ourselves and fast individually and also as a nation?

• When you want a breakthrough. Revival is always needed in Christianity. We all get complacent and do not always do what we should be doing before the Lord. Revival does just what it says: it revives us. Maybe we should all be fasting for a spiritual revival for Christians everywhere.

---

63 Matthew 17:21
64 Joel 1:14
65 Psalm 51

When you do fast, keep your cool. Jesus says to not let anyone else know you are fasting. Sometimes I don't even mention to my wife that I am fasting until she rings the dinner bell. Then the cat is out of the bag, and I confess I can't eat tonight, thanks, though. She is good at accepting this. Keep your physical appearance normal so no one knows you are fasting. Don't put yourself in a spot where you reveal you are on a fast. Be humble and quiet about it.[66]

I remember learning that the two most powerful urges of the human body are eating and sex, with eating being number one. Some people are addicted to various sins and have a hard time overcoming them. Fasting is a good spiritual discipline to help overcome sin. If you can overcome eating through your fasting and praying, then this will help you overcome your other weaknesses, too. If you are struggling with a particular addiction that may need professional help, ask your pastor for guidance and seek professional help.

Don't think that fasting is going to cause God to act and that what you are seeking will be a done deal. If you go in with that attitude, you have lost the battle already. A fast is only asking God to consider your petition. We need to be extremely humble, cry out, wail. Put ash on your head, put on sackcloth, lay low when you fast, and pray to the Lord.[67] Attitude is the key word here. If your heart is not in it, then neither is God's. Remember, God always answers prayer on His timetable, not ours. His timetable is always perfect. He considers our wholeness, not just the prayer. His ways are perfect, so be patient. Humble yourself when you fast and pray. Develop a fasting program to draw you closer to God.

66 Matthew 6:16-18
67 Joel 2:12; Jonah 3:5-9

Chapter 14

Be Disciplined

"Enter through the narrow gate. For wide is the gate and broad is the way that leads to destruction, and many enter through it. But small is the gate and narrow the way that leads to life, and only a few find it."

Matthew 7:13-14

How do you practice walking the narrow way to salvation? Do you have a plan to keep yourself up to date and current with the Holy Spirit? Well, I could say practicing the Four Commands of Christ is one way, but you still have to be disciplined. One thing that "the days of Noah" and this present day have in common is apathy. Apathy is the spiritual cancer of the human race right now. Not very many of us are willing to spend the time it takes to be successful in our relationship with God. Some of us become discouraged and quit, and others of us just don't try very hard in the first place.

Let's return to Mark's retelling of Jesus's parable about sowing seeds:

Listen! A farmer went out to sow his seed. As he was scattering the seed, some fell along the path, and the birds came and ate it up. Some fell on rocky places, where it did not have much soil. It sprang up quickly because the soil was shallow. But when the sun came up, the plants were scorched, and they withered because they had no root. Other seed fell among thorns, which grew up and choked the plants, so that they did not bear grain. Still other seed fell on good soil. It came up, grew and produced a crop, some multiplying thirty, some sixty, some a hundred times. (Mark 4:3-8)

Jesus shares with us how humanity reacts to His gospel. I would like to put numbers to this to show you how important it is to make sure you are anchored in Christ. In the Parable of the Sower, there are four examples of the Word being sowed. Only a fraction of the seeds are actually able to take root. Bringing this to bear on our own lives and salvation, what are we to do? We need to change our habits and start working on a plan to stay close to Christ until He returns. Let's look at some possibilities:

1. Use the Spiritual Disciplines in the Four Commands of Christ as your basis of study.

2. Memorize the Four Commands of Christ.

3. Set goals to accomplish the Spiritual Disciplines in your spiritual formation and daily walk.

4. Make sure you are part of a church and in a small group.

5. Memorize the Apostles' Creed.

6. Surround yourself with good Christian mentors.

What are some of the characteristics of discipline? How do we develop these characteristics of discipline? Set goals for each habit you wish to change or adopt and work your plan. Take one at a time and work on it for six weeks.

- Persevering
- Having good habits
- Staying focused
- Being willing to adapt
- Setting and working towards goals
- Keeping a good attitude

Most people think of discipline as punishment; while that can be true, let us think of it as a way to change our habits, to train ourselves with exercises in self-control to improve our mental faculties and moral character. Self-control, what a concept! I am not sure how many of us have practiced self-control. If you look at society and how people have been living recently, it seems uncontrolled: partying at colleges, Mardi Gras, prostitution around big events like the Super Bowl. The lasciviousness present at these settings is unbelievable. People are willing to do just about anything to fill in the lonely gap that they have inside them due to a lack of direction, moral character, and the Holy Spirit. As a nation, we have locked out any Godly influences on our children, teens, and adults. We can no longer even display the Ten Commandments in any government institution. This shows that our children are definitely not being brought up disciplined, especially when it comes to moral character.

Where does morality come from? When we talk about morality, we must include virtues. Virtues define what moral road we take based upon our adoptions of each virtue. Everyone has a compass—moral character—they use to guide them through this life. Some acquire it from their parents, some from school, and some from friends. We know from Romans that each individual is born with a Godly moral character. It gets skewed based upon the teaching from either their parents or acquaintances. They adopt their surroundings: *"Teach a child in the way they should go, and they will never depart from it"* (Proverbs 22:6).

Virtues are not taught in schools anymore, nor are the stories of virtues lived out. Church is the only place you can get God's moral virtues. If only 22 percent[68] of America is going to church, then we as a nation are losing the battle of truth. Jesus said, *"I am the way and the truth"* (John 14:6a). After Pilate asked Him if He was a king, Jesus also said, *"For this reason I was born and have come into the world, to testify to the truth"* (John 18:37). Truth. There it is. All of us on this Earth are lost without God's Truth.

Jesus is God's truth. Jesus is our moral compass. When we adopt Jesus into our lives, truth comes alive within us, a truth so powerful that the world does not understand, but we do. Truth is everlasting. It has been written on man's heart from the beginning of time, and the only reason we cannot see it in others is because they have hardened themselves to it. This is where anger and misguided conduct come from. The virtues of truth and God's holy laws are also very helpful in our body. When someone lies all the time, they do not know what truth is, their mind gets skewed with heaviness of heart, and stress breaks the body down. Just saying, truth will set you free.

Truth is manifested in many ways. One way is Godly virtues. Even the ancients wanted to study this topic. Honesty, compassion, integrity, perseverance, chastity, purity, and thankfulness are just some of the many virtues. It takes discipline, though, to exude these in your everyday life. I have coined the parable of the narrow passage as discipline, and the reason is because it takes discipline to maintain your relationship with Christ. Without Christ, you will never be able to attain a lasting truth. The world's truth is a lie. Christ brought truth to the world for whosoever will accept it. You can come up with all the lies that are being tossed around by the world on your own, but the lies of the world are so bad that they are willing to punish anyone who disagrees with them. Now you should be aware of why Christ was killed upon a cross: to squash the truth.

So, now that we have accepted Jesus into our life, how do we continue in our spiritual growth? Discipline needs to be part of your spiritual

---

68 • Church attendance of Americans 2021 | Statista

formation to be a successful Christian. Disciplined to read your bible, disciplined to pray, disciplined to fast, disciplined to witness to others and become a mentor. I have always asked students of mine to set goals for themselves and to set the First Command of Christ as their governing value. Accept Jesus into your heart and become disciplined in your actions according to Christ's teaching, and your load will be lifted, and you will inherit the right to live with Christ forever.

Chapter 15

Find Strength in Your Weakness

"Therefore, in order to keep me from becoming conceited,
I was given a thorn in my flesh, a messenger of Satan, to
torment me. Three times I pleaded with the Lord to take it
away from me. But he said to me, 'My grace is sufficient for
you, for my power is made perfect in weakness.' Therefore, I
will boast all the more gladly about my weaknesses, so that
Christ's power may rest on me. That is why, for Christ's sake,
I delight in weaknesses, in insults, in hardships, in persecutions,
in difficulties. For when I am weak, then I am strong."

2 Corinthians 12:7-10

For years, I have wondered what the story of Paul and the thorn means. I have come to the conclusion that we are closer to Jesus when we are in the height of our trials, no matter what those trials may be. John would not have been able to write the Book of Revelation if he were sitting somewhere in comfort and had all he needed. He may not have moved forward with the revelation of Jesus without the experience of isolation that the prison island Patmos provided. We all need something in our life that gives us a push forward in our faith. In tragedy, we reach out to Jesus and draw closer to God.

Is there something you won't release to Jesus? A hidden sin, an anger issue, someone you won't forgive? I know people who are mad at God or blame God for the loss of a loved one, not realizing that it keeps them from being filled with the Spirit and unable to move forward in their growth. Sampson experienced this. He knew what a Nazarite vow was and knew he was to keep this vow, yet he let himself be taken in by his sin nature. The message is the same to us as it was to them: Overcome your deficiencies and be victorious. Anyone who will allow his heart and soul to listen to Christ's criticism will overcome and be victorious. This is what John wrote in Revelations 3:21, *"To the one who is victorious, I will give the right to sit with me on my throne, just as I was victorious and sat down with my Father on his throne."* When you have issues that are hard to overcome, put these issues in front of Christ. Leave them there on the proverbial altar and let God fight the battle that is inside of you.

What does it take to overcome our old ways and accept Christ's commands so we can be counted with the elect, accept Jesus Christ as our savior, and live according to His Scriptures? Get on your knees every morning and ask Christ to heal your heart and soul. Ask for forgiveness for the beam in your heart (eye). When released, pray for others. He says He will fight our battle and give us peace, His peace, *Shalom Adonai*. Christ says that, for those of us who will overcome, He will give us clothes befitting of a royal marriage, and our names will be written in the Book of Life forever. Is this such a hard price to pay to spend time with our Lord? Let's change our ways and let Jesus do His miracles in us.

Consider taking a sabbatical to find Christ. Some have gone off to a deserted area and fasted and prayed for a time. Some have immersed themselves into prayer vigils. Do whatever it takes to find Christ. I use the Four Commands of Christ to center myself and my governing values to govern me. I get on my knees and ask God to cover me with His righteousness (blood), and I bask in that. I listen to great Christian music that I am blessed with on the radio and on YouTube.

One thing I do know is that, if you have any maturity in the Lord, spread His gospel in any way you can. Pray for people you know are lost. Invite them to either accept Jesus and or come to your church to hear the Word. Believe me, they want to be found. They want to know there is something out there that is better than where they are now. They all want grace and mercy—just like us. We all want grace and mercy from our neighbor, but especially from God. Let your neighbor know what it means to be filled with the Holy Spirit.

Since you have kept my command to endure patiently, I will also keep you from the hour of trial that is going to come on the whole world to test the inhabitants of the earth. I am coming soon. Hold on to what you have, so that no one will take your crown. The one who is victorious I will make a pillar in the temple of my God. Never again will they leave it. I will write on them the name of my God and the name of the city of my God, the new Jerusalem, which is coming down out of heaven from my God; and I will also write on them my new name. Whoever has ears, let them hear what the Spirit says to the churches. (Revelation 3:10-13)

It is because of this time in history that God decided to give the Four Commands of Christ to the world. He is telling us to concentrate on His Four Commands and overcome the world. I have had enough medical operations to know the pain that we all go through when we are in the hour of trial. Pain leads to healing; it is always darkest before the dawn. I know the pain of life can become unbearable, and some may want solitude in these moments, but maybe the best time to share Christ is when you are at your lowest. Giving to others will create joy in your heart. It is better to give than to receive. One aspect of man's nature is to help others in need without any expectations of receiving it back. When life has us cornered and we can see no way out, this is the time to surrender. Surrender your heart and problems to Jesus. He doesn't always take away the situation we are in, but He definitely walks through it with us. We can find joy and peace if we seek Him.

Remember what the early Christians went through during persecution of their faith. They were murdered, fed to the lions, burned at the stake, boiled, and set upon the cross to die. We have not seen any of that in our lifetime, yet. Wars and rumors of wars are becoming more and more prevalent. People endure many hardships, but Christ is there for those who seek Him out. Some of the greatest stories of faith come out of these hardships. Christ will raise you up.

Chapter 16

Examine Yourself

A re you searching your soul to find out who you really are? Do you know what you believe? How do you live your life? Are you allowing worldly ways into your life? Is there a paradigm or dogma that drives you? Man has always wanted to know if there is more to life than what he is currently seeing and living, especially if he is in the fast lane and never had training in the way of our Lord Jesus Christ. We need to examine ourselves because humans have the propensity to stray and replace truth with a lie. Look at Adam and Eve for an example of this.[69]

So many philosophies and religions have tackled this subject throughout history. Some say you need to find your chi, some say to do yoga, some say to sacrifice and live frugally, some say to meditate. Each religion has a way to achieve what they believe is a good way. There is one virtue that most religions end up having in common: the Golden Rule. Everyone wants to be treated with fairness, to be shown grace and mercy. Each religion teaches this differently, yet if you look closely, you will see that there is some truth in most of them. This truth gets skewed from thousands of years of sin in man who is trying to figure things out without the influence of the one true God. Their teachings have become so out of touch with the creator that people become lost. In no other religion did the gods walk the earth, sacrifice themselves for humanity, and rise from the dead so we could have forgiveness

---

69 Genesis 3:1-20

of our sins. No other religion sent a helper, the Holy Spirit. No other religion's god could calm a storm, heal lepers, or remove evil spirits.

The God of Creation knew what our thoughts, lives, and religions would be at this very time during this age. Man has very seldom stayed the course in believing in the one true God. Man has strayed and brought in myths to soothe his soul. Who really holds the key? To make sure after the flood that man would have a record of who YHWH is, He chose a man named Abram to follow Him.

The God of heaven chose Abraham to be the father of all of us who believe in the one true God and gave Abraham and his descendants the Promised Land. This land was called "promised" because He did not let Abraham own it yet, as the people who lived there at the time had not reached their full sin yet.[70] The covenant between God and Abraham and Abraham's descendants was signed by the act of circumcision. The Promised Land passed from Abraham to Isaac, then from Isaac to Jacob, whose name was changed to Israel, then to Moses, who led Israel out of slavery in Egypt to the very edge of the Promised Land. Jesus came to fulfill this promise by showing us the way to the heavenly promised land, heaven. Jesus came to bring truth to the world and bring about a change in man's behavior.

Jesus made this salvation easy for all and also made it simple: just believe in Him. God has always had requirements for how we are to live and behave while we are here on this earth. After the flood, God gave His decrees and laws to the patriarchs through Moses. He gave them the Ten Commandments and requirements to have sin abolished out of their lives. Even with the Law given by God to the Israelites, they still sinned. So, God made a way to nullify sin's effect on them by sacrificing animals to Him. Knowing that more was needed, He sent His son to be the final sacrifice for our sins. Paul explains it well in Hebrews 10:1-2:

> *For the law is only a shadow of the good things to come, not*
> *the realities themselves. It can never, by the same sacrifices*

---

70 Genesis 15:16

offered year after year, make perfect those who draw near
to worship. If it could, would not the offerings have ceased?
For the worshipers would have been cleansed once for all
and would no longer have felt the guilt of their sins.

Jesus is the final sacrifice needed for our sins. He has paid the price once and for all for you and me. Now, since you are alive at this time in history, you have choices to make in your life. The most important choice is where your eternal soul will live. The Israelites had issues throughout their history regarding which dogma to follow. They could follow the true God who saved them from Egypt and gave them a land to call their own—or they could follow the gods of Egypt. Joshua also gave them a choice to make just before they crossed into the Promised Land:

But if serving the LORD seems undesirable to you, then choose
for yourselves this day whom you will serve, whether the gods
your ancestors served beyond the Euphrates, or the gods of the
Amorites, in whose land you are living. But as for me and my
household, we will serve the LORD. (Joshua 24:15)

Who will you choose? God has given humanity free will, meaning you can decide which direction you may want to go with your life. As Christians, we must follow Christ's teachings, and you can decide to do the same by being born again. Jesus has made His commandments easy and concise. These have been summarized in The Four Commands of Christ so that they are not difficult to grasp. No deep discernment is needed. Just humble yourself and submit to His commands. Surrender. Jesus says, *"If you love me, keep my commands"* (John 14:15). If you submit to these Four Commands and follow the instructions for them, you will become a successful Christian. But if you water them down with your own interpretations and go the way of the world, you will be in trouble. God has given us a way for to test ourselves to see if we are in His will. I ask you to examine yourself while contemplating the following quotes:

The unexamined life is not worth living. (Socrates)

Everyone ought to examine themselves before they eat of the bread and drink from the cup.(1 Corinthians 11:28)

Examine yourselves to see whether you are in the faith; test yourselves. Can't you see for yourselves that Jesus Christ is in you—unless you actually fail the test? (2 Corinthians 13:5)

What shall we say then? Shall we continue in sin, that grace may abound? God forbid. How shall we, that are dead to sin, live any longer therein? Know ye not, that so many of us as were baptized into Jesus Christ were baptized into his death? Therefore, we are buried with him by baptism into death: that like as Christ was raised up from the dead by the glory of the Father, even so we also should walk in newness of life. (Romans 6:1-4)

If we deliberately go on sinning after we have received the knowledge of the truth, no further sacrifice for sins remains, but only a fearful expectation of judgment and of raging fire that will consume all adversaries. Anyone who rejected the law of Moses died without mercy on the testimony of two or three witnesses. How much more severely do you think one deserves to be punished who has trampled on the Son of God, profaned the blood of the covenant that sanctified him, and insulted the Spirit of grace? (Hebrews 10:26-29)

I am sure you are asking yourself—and me—by now: how do I examine myself? How do I know if I am in the faith? I have thought about this a lot also and have used this examination process for myself and shared it with others. I know some of you are saying to yourself under your breath: "He can't tell me who I am and whom I will serve.

He is judging me!" I am telling you I don't judge you, but your fruits judge you. What are the fruits you are putting forth in the world?

> *By their fruit you will recognize them. Do people pick grapes from thornbushes, or figs from thistles? Likewise, every good tree bears good fruit, but a bad tree bears bad fruit. (Matthew 7:16)*

> *Even a young man is known by his actions—whether his conduct is pure and upright. (Proverbs 20:11)*

> *For each tree is known by its own fruit. Indeed, people do not gather figs from thornbushes, or grapes from brambles. (Luke 6:44)*

> *But someone will say, "You have faith and I have deeds." Show me your faith without deeds, and I will show you my faith by my deeds. (James 2:18)*

You can see in the Scriptures from the Old Testament to the New Testament that we are to bear good fruits pleasing to the Lord. The Word of God (Jesus) was present during King David's time and continued with the discipling of Christ's apostles. This requirement to bear good fruit passed from the apostles to us.

I will be honest—the thought of tackling "examination of oneself" in this book was a hard decision. Then God sent me the message I needed to hear. One Sunday, I was reminded about the need to wait on the Lord in a sermon about David. I knew those words concerned my writing of this book. The preacher, one of the general superintendents of my Church, discussed David's inquiring of the Lord before making major decisions for Israel and himself. David inquired of the Lord nine times, and each time he waited for an answer from the Lord. At each inquiry, God gave him instruction on what to do and how to overcome the inquiry that he had made. I had fasted that week, looking for an answer from God as to whether this was the right time to publish this book and who the publisher should be.

That Sunday, I received the message to wait. So, I prayed for weeks about why I was to wait. To be frank, the last month had not gone well for me. Nothing seemed to work in my favor. I was kind of wondering where God was in all this. I assumed He would lead me in a direction and give me the reason for waiting. It did not come right away, as it did for David, and my world did not fall apart. I had bad news about my health, finances, and relationships. When I wanted to share the Four Commands with people and churches, doors were shut. I assumed everyone would want to hear about the good news from Jesus! I wondered if I'd done something wrong. Then, one day, I was reading Galatians 5:13-26, where Paul states to live by the spirit and not by the flesh. God opened my thoughts to this as a way to test my spirit. I am asking the question now: are we living to satisfy the flesh, or are we living to satisfy the spirit? Or, God forbid, are we living in both?

After examining myself, I was comforted to know that I am aligned with Christ. I am now asking all of you to test your spirit, too. See if you are living according to God's requirements. What are they? Use Galatians 5:22-26 to see if this is the behavior that you are showing to your family and the world. Use Galatians 5:19-21 to see if you are "not" in the Spirit but in the flesh. If you have any of these habits or traits listed in verses 19 through 21, then you need to get on your knees and ask God to forgive you and renew your mind. Then I would consult with your pastor and make yourself available for accountability. All of us should be open to accountability with our brothers in Christ.

How do we fix the problem? Start by asking Jesus to forgive fleshly habits, renew your mind, and give you a steadfast heart. Memorize Galatians 5:22-26 so you know what good behavior looks like. Continue with 1 Corinthians 13:4-13. This way you will know what "love" (Agape) really looks like. Follow and adopt the Four Commands of Christ into your life. Humble yourself and submit. Give your neighbor, spouse, and children grace and mercy. Forgive your fellow members of your church or others if you are holding a grudge against them; do not harbor ill feelings, or bitterness, no matter what.[71] As you go along in life, go and tell people about Christ and what He has done in your life.

After you have worked on the above, start every day on your knees next to your bed. Read the Bible every day. Do this and know Christ is with you all the way. Paul states perseverance is the key to success. Do not give Satan an inch. Don't allow bad language or foul thoughts to enter your mind or come out of your mouth. Do not give fodder to your natural desires. Do not allow yourself to be caught up in gossip either. If you feel something has penetrated your defenses, cut it off immediately. Go to your pastor and mentors and ask for help. A praying church is a living church. When you are aligned with Christ, practice intercessory prayer for all who need Christ. Ask anything and Jesus will answer. I call this being in the zone.

> *Finally, be strong in the Lord and in His mighty power.*
> *Put on the full armor of God, so that you can make your*
> *stand against the devil's schemes. For our struggle is not*
> *against flesh and blood, but against the rulers, against the*
> *authorities, against the powers of this world's darkness, and*
> *against the spiritual forces of evil in the heavenly realms.*
> *(Ephesians 6:10-12)*

By applying the Four Commands of Christ and the spiritual disciplines to your life, you will succeed as a Christian.

---

71 John 4:13-14

Conclusion

Pﾠeople have struggled for generations with how to get Christianity correct. Thousands of books have been written on how to get close and stay close to God. In Exodus 18:20, Jethro said to Moses, *"Teach them His decrees and instructions, and show them the way they are to live and how they are to behave."* God wants all of you reading this to know His words are as true today as they were in Moses's day. Hearken to them, I am pleading with you. Christ gave us the Four Commands as a package of simplistic teaching to show us His will. What is Jesus's will for us?

*If you keep my commands, you will remain in my love, just
as I have kept my Father's commands and remain in his
love. (John 15:10)*

If you love me, you will keep my commands. (John 14:15)

*Then Jesus came to them and said, "All authority in heaven
and on earth has been given to me. Therefore, go and make
disciples of all nations, baptizing them in the name of the
Father and of the Son and of the Holy Spirit, and teaching
them to obey everything I have commanded you. And surely
I am with you always, to the very end of the age." (Matthew
28:18-20)*

When you read these Scripture passages, you have to ask yourself: do I keep His commandments, and am I obeying His voice? If you follow the Four Commands of Christ, you will find Jesus in a way you didn't think possible. A lot of people lack the mindset of due diligence to stay in the relationship or to be holy. Apathy seems to have ruled the day! Jesus didn't die on the cross for us to fail. Shall we continue in sin? No!

> *Now may the God of peace, who through the blood of the eternal covenant brought back from the dead our Lord Jesus, that great Shepherd of the sheep, equip you with every good thing to do His will. And may He accomplish in us what is pleasing in His sight through Jesus Christ, to whom be glory forever and ever. Amen. (Hebrews 13:20-21)*

We can see from these scriptures that we need to be equipped with every good thing to do His will, and the Four Commands of Christ do just that if you apply them to your life.

We all face these questions at one point or time in our life: who am I? Do I have purpose? Where am I going? What is my mission in life? How am I going to get there? Am I okay in my relationship with Christ, or do I need to improve? Through the power of the Holy Spirit, we can be a holy people. The Four Commands of Christ are about anchoring your relationship with Christ as you work your way toward Christian perfection. Remember that your faults, if taken to Christ, are covered by His blood. There is nothing you have done that Christ will not forgive, except one thing: your continuance of a hard heart and refuse to change.

Your purpose in life is to glorify God. Your mission in life is to spread the Gospel as you go along in life. Your main goal in life is Christian perfection, holy living. This book, if applied, will get you there.

www.ingramcontent.com/pod-product-compliance
Lightning Source LLC
Chambersburg PA
CBHW070717130626
46553CB00005B/2034